THE Newfoundland Rangers

**Compiled by Darrin McGrath, Robert Smith,
Rangers Ches Parsons and Norman Crane**

Library and Archives Canada Cataloguing in Publication

The Newfoundland Rangers / Darrin McGrath ... [et al.].

ISBN 0-9684209-9-0

Canadian Cataloguing in Publication Data
1. Newfoundland Ranger Force--History. 2. Police--Newfoundland and Labrador--History.
HV8159.N5N49 2005   363.2'09718
C2005-906924-4

Front cover photograph first group of 30 Rangers with Chief Ranger Leonard Stick. Underneath, site of the first Ranger headquarters in Whitbourne.

DRC Publishing

3 Parliament Street
St. John's, NL, A1A 2Y6

Phone 726-0960
E-mail staceypj@nfld.com

Dedication

This book is dedicated to all the men who served in the Newfoundland Rangers, especially Daniel Corcoran (Number 14), Michael Greene (No. 49) and Michael Collins (No. 166), all of whom died while on duty.

ACKNOWLEDGEMENTS

First and foremost, this book would not have been possible without the research of Ches Parsons. His determination and drive helped ensure the completion of the book. Ches was a workhorse in digging up information on deceased Rangers.

Thanks also to Norm Crane for his work in helping create the book, especially in obtaining photos. There were many meetings at Norm's house concerning this book. No doubt Norm's wife Penney will be happy to see this project completed.

Norm and Ches did the basic research, I wrote the findings up.

Thanks to Ranger George Pauls.

Provincial Court Judge Robert Smith also played a key role in this project. In fact, the book was his idea. He and his wife, Ella Hiscock, proofread the manuscript.

Thanks to Peter and Jean Stacey of DRC Publishing for their scholarship, their careful attention to detail, their generous advice and assistance in turning this book into a form that pleases the surviving Rangers.

Thanks to Dianne Lynch for the excellent cover design and lay-out.

I also want to thank my wife Ann for her unwavering love and support.

A big thanks to Vince Hempsall and Ron Young at The Downhomer magazine for running an excerpt from the book in their September 2005 issue.

Thanks to Peter Jackson of The Telegram newspaper for his interest in the Ranger history and for publishing the story of Ranger Tom Curnew.

Thanks to Jim Wellman of The Navigator magazine which I write for each month. Likewise many thanks to Tim Hickey of Columbia magazine.

The City of St. John's provided a small Arts Grant towards this project and that financial support is appreciated.

Kevin Alyward and William R. Callahan were a big help in the early days of this project and their assistance is deeply appreciated.

Thanks to all the Rangers, wives, widows and children of Rangers who helped out with this book especially: Bob Dingwall, Gerry Curnew, Christine O'Halleran, Hannah Ryan, Sister Marie Ryan.

Last, but certainly not least, it is important to acknowledge that the wives of all the Rangers played a big role in their husbands' careers and thus this book. Wives acted as "unofficial" Rangers and often had to put up with sharing accommodations with prisoners or mental patients.

Darrin McGrath
St. John's, Newfoundland
October 2005

TABLE OF CONTENTS

~ *Chapter* **1** *One* ~

INTRODUCTION

"Ranger, Ranger, you better come quick! Esau Gillingham is going to shoot the railway agent," the young boy exclaimed as he threw open the door to the Ranger station in Glenwood.

Ranger Norman "Norm" Crane jumped to his feet and pulled on his jacket and service revolver. "The west-bound train had come through Glenwood that night and Gillingham must have been on-board," Crane thought to himself as he hurried towards the railway station. Esau Gillingham was a trapper born in the Gambo area in 1877, and he was well-known as a drinker and all-around "hard ticket." He was the "White Eskimo" of Harold Horwood's book of the same name.

When the Ranger arrived at the station he found Gillingham, wearing a mackinaw jacket, waving a rifle and threatening to kill the station agent for robbing two bottles of his rum. With his unkempt, grey hair and fiery eyes, Gillingham cut an imposing figure.

"Without drawing my revolver, I confronted Gillingham and demanded he give me the rifle, which he did without protest. I determined he believed the station agent had stolen two bottles of rum, when in fact the rum had been over-carried to the Norris Arm station and would arrive back in Glenwood on the next east-bound train," Crane says.

Ranger Crane assured the trapper the missing alcohol would turn up and the man quieted down and went to his lodgings. The next day Crane returned the rifle to Gillingham and no charges were laid. "He promised to be of good behavior while in the Glenwood area," Crane recalls with a smile.

The foregoing story is a good example of how the Newfoundland Rangers operated. Ranger Crane never drew his service revolver when confronting the armed Gillingham and managed to diffuse the escalating situation with courtesy, common sense and courage. The episode was resolved with no charges laid and an eventual apology from Gillingham. No doubt such interactions steeped the high esteem with which the Rangers were held.

As Ranger Ron Peet told Harold Horwood: "We (Rangers) were peace officers, putting more emphasis on peace than police." Common sense, courtesy and taking the highroad were the basic tools of the Ranger more so than guns and grit.

An anecdote from Ches Parsons highlights the relationship between the residents of small outport villages and the Ranger. Ranger Parsons was stationed on the south coast when he received a report that a group of fishermen had just landed a lot of French contraband liquor. He jumped on the motorcycle that was equipped with a sidecar and began speeding to the outport in question. Keep in mind that this was in the days before helmet-safety was practiced.

"I was speeding along and because of the sidecar I lost control of the vehicle when I was taking a corner. The next thing I knew I was in a bog," Ches says.

Shortly after the crash, a car came along driven by a local Doctor. Once the physician found the Ranger was unhurt, he drove into town to get some help to get the motorcycle back on the road.

"The Doctor came back with the very men I was going to investigate for rum-running. They helped pull the motorcycle out of the bog and onto the road. One of the men joked to me that, 'You won't catch us today, Ranger,'" Ches recalls.

The townspeople knew the Ranger was out to catch smugglers but they were not beyond helping him out when he was in a jam. Such was the respect and regard that outport Newfoundlanders bestowed upon the Rangers.

A BRIEF HISTORY OF RANGERS

The Newfoundland Rangers were created in 1935 under the six-man Commission of Government that ruled Newfoundland from 1933 - 1949.

The first Rangers went into the field in 1935, so 2005 marks the 70th anniversary of that event. While the Rangers policed outport areas, they were more than just policemen, a point Cyril Goodyear makes in his book "The Road to Nowhere."

The first Ranger (former Newfoundland Constabulary member Brian White) was recruited on July 9, 1935, and by the end of that month, thirty men had been sworn in as Rangers.

The Rangers were modeled after the Royal Canadian Mounted Police (RCMP) and were intended to supplement the mainly urban-based Newfoundland Constabulary. The first Rangers were trained for three months in Whitbourne by members of the RCMP. Their uniform closely resembled the Mounties' garb; khaki jacket and wide-legged breeches with a brown stripe, knee-high brown field boots and a khaki cap. The Rangers' badge was a solid brass disc adorned with a caribou head and inscribed with the words "Newfoundland Rangers."

The uniform had a rather militarized-appearance and Rangers were trained in a para-military style which included marching drill, infantry drill, small arms and rifle instruction. They were instructed to always keep themselves neat and tidy and to treat the public with respect at all times. They were, after all, the only representatives of government most outport Newfoundlanders would ever see.

The first Chief Ranger was Leonard Stick who held the distinction of being regimental Number One in the Newfoundland Regiment in the First World War. According to Harold Horwood, Stick was commissioned an officer during the battle of Beaumont Hamel on July 1, 1916.

As Chief Ranger, Stick held the rank of Major, while his second-in-command, R.D.Fraser (another WW I army officer) held the rank of Inspector.

According to Horwood, the actual training was in the hands of Sgt. Major Fred Anderton who had been seconded from the RCMP for a period of two years. Anderton followed Stick as the second Chief Ranger.

E.W. Greenley was the third Chief Ranger followed by R.D.Fraser. Edward L. Martin came up through the ranks to serve as Chief from 1943 to 1950, when the Force was disbanded.

In terms of recruitment, the Rangers had their pick of the cream of the crop of Newfoundland's young men. Candidates had to possess at least a grade eleven education, a high standard in the 1930s. The minimum age was supposed to be 19, but there were cases when underage men entered the Rangers. For example, George Pauls became a Ranger before he had turned eighteen.

The Newfoundland Rangers were an attractive career choice for educated Newfoundlanders at a time when good, paid work was hard to come by. Rangers were provided with board and lodging and full uniforms, including undergarments.

According to Horwood, first class Rangers earned $2 per day, second class earned $1.75, while third class rangers earned $1.50. Sergeants made $3 a day or $1,095 per year. That was considered big money in those days.

The Chief Ranger made the princely sum of $2,100, with the entire budget for fifty-one Rangers in 1937 being $40,000, says Norman Crane.

So attractive was the Ranger lifestyle that at least twenty-two members of the Newfoundland Constabulary transferred to the Rangers.

The Rangers were attached to the Commission of Government's Department of Natural Resources but they enforced laws of all six departments of the Commission.

Under Finance Department regulations, the Rangers collected custom duties and acted as wreck commissioners. In the realm of Natural Resources the Rangers enforced game laws, inspected logging camps and fought fires.

In terms of the Department of Justice, the Rangers enforced criminal laws and investigated suspicious deaths. With regards the Home Affairs and Education Department, Rangers acted as truant officers and organized adult education programs. In relation to the Public Utilities Department, Rangers supervised the maintenance and construction of roads, wharves and breakwaters.

Perhaps the most difficult task facing the Rangers came under the umbrella of the Public Health and Welfare Department of Commission Government. Essentially, they acted as welfare officers in outport areas and had to issue relief payments (i.e. welfare). Recall that this was during the "dirty thirties" when the Great Depression raged. Much of outport Newfoundland was impoverished and deciding who was to receive welfare was a difficult task.

As part of their duties under the Health and Welfare Department, Rangers were also charged with escorting the mentally ill to hospital in St. John's. Patients sometimes had to be fitted with straight-jackets.

4

On one occasion a Ranger was escorting a mentally ill person to St. John's on the trans-island train long before the days of the Trans-Canada Highway. The patient began to get upset causing a ruckus on the train. In an effort to quiet the person, the Ranger began to sing to him. The patient quieted down, and when the Ranger finished singing, the patient promised to be of good behavior if the Ranger promised to not sing anymore.

When the Second World War started, the Rangers took on extra duties of patrolling coast-lines and keeping their eyes open for suspicious activities. Rangers on the Labrador coast kept a watchful eye out for enemy submarines and ships. When the passenger ferry Caribou was torpedoed in the Gulf of St. Lawrence in October 1942, Rangers assisted with retrieval and burial of victims. The Rangers also assisted with the rescue of American sailors from the U.S. Navy ships Truxton and Pollux which went ashore near Lawn, Placentia Bay, in February 1942.

Perhaps one of the most important functions of the Rangers was to act as mediator between outport communities and the Commission of Government. Under the Commission, no elections were held and so there were no democratically selected members to represent the interests of outport citizens.

For example, Ranger Jarvis was serving in Lanse au Clair, Labrador, in 1947 when he met an elderly gentleman seeking welfare relief. The Ranger noticed the man's right arm was crippled and upon inquiry learned the man was a veteran of WWI and had been wounded in action but never received a pension. So Ranger Jarvis began the journey through the red tape and regulations to assist the man to receive the war pension he so rightly deserved.

In 1949, when Newfoundland joined Canada, the death knell for the Newfoundland Rangers was sounded. As a sign of the high esteem in which they were held, Rangers were given the opportunity to join the RCMP. A total of 55 Rangers transferred to the RCMP. Six of those men attained officer's rank and twenty-four were promoted to Senior Non-Commissioned Officer rank up to Sgt.-Major.

Not only did the former Rangers distinguish themselves in service as members of the RCMP, but many of them also went on to make significant contributions in the provincial civil service. Ches Parsons has determined at least six Magistrates came from the ranks of the Rangers. Rangers also went on to serve as Chief Warden at the Penitentiary, Chief Game Warden for the Province, Auditor General, Registrar of the Supreme Court, Provincial Archivist and High Sheriff. One Ranger, Cyril Goodyear, has written four books.

At least two former Rangers, William Smith and Samuel Drover, were elected to the House of Assembly as MHA's. Drover was first elected as a

Liberal, but then he left Premier Smallwood's caucus and sat as a member of the CCF (Cooperative Commonwealth Federation) the first member of the party in this province. The CCF was the predecessor of the NDP.

William Smith, a lawyer, holds the distinction of being the first member of the Progressive Conservative Party elected in outport Newfoundland. Before Smith's election, the Smallwood Liberals held a stranglehold on outport Newfoundland voters.

Three members of the Rangers died in the execution of their duties: #14 Danny Corcoran, #49 Michael Greene, and #166 Michael Collins.

Corcoran died in St. Anthony hospital after getting lost on the open barrens of the Great Northern Peninsula while on patrol in March 1936. His saga is recounted in the moving epic "Will Anyone Search for Danny?" by retired game warden Earl Pilgrim.

Michael Greene met his end when his horse and sleigh broke through the ice of a pond near Lamaline on the Burin Peninsula in 1940. He apparently managed to get out of the water but perished nearby from exposure.

Young Michael Collins died tragically when the motorcycle he was driving went off the road near Stephenville in 1945. Another Ranger traveling in the sidecar, Expedite Howard, was uninjured.

Between 1935 and 1950, a total of 204 men served as Rangers. But at any one time, the entire complement of Rangers in the field never exceeded 72 men. Of the 204 men, 80 of the Rangers had less than five years service, while nine members had six months service or less. Only seven served for the fifteen years of the Force's existence.

Regimental numbers 81 - 90 were Supernumerary Members engaged for special duty, guarding installations in the new airport at Gander during WWII. Most of these Supernumerary Rangers served less than one year, while a couple did engage for five year terms.

Thirty-four of the men who served as Rangers also answered the call to arms in the Second World War. When hostilities broke out in 1939, Rangers enlisted in all branches of the armed services from the Canadian Navy, British Navy, Royal Air Force, Royal Canadian Air Force to the Newfoundland Heavy Artillery. In fact, Norman Crane says that the very existence of the Rangers was threatened with the mass resignations to enter the armed services. Therefore, the British Dominions office designated Rangers as an essential service and discharges for the purposes of enlistment were disallowed.

At least four of the 204 Rangers became clergymen after leaving the force. They are # 7 Leslie Chaffey; # 83 John MacDonald; # 148 Kevin Ryan; and # 189 John Murdoch. No doubt the desire to serve their fellow man that had helped draw them into the Rangers also drew them to answer a greater calling.

Another interesting fact about the Rangers is that there were sixteen sets of brothers who served as Rangers. For example, Joe Delahunty (# 9) was in the first group of Rangers, while his brother Michael (# 40) was in the second group to train.

Two members of the Newfoundland Rangers were awarded the King's Police and Fire Service Medal for Gallantry; # 79 Corporal John Hogan and # 107 Bruce Gillingham.

John Hogan was decorated following an episode in which he parachuted out of a smoke-filled plane over the wilderness of the Northern Peninsula in 1943. Hogan stayed with his badly injured companion, Corporal Butt of the Air Force, and kept him alive for seven weeks until they were rescued.

Similarly, Bruce Gillingham was decorated for his apprehension of a rifle-toting killer in Norris Arm in 1948. The gunman had shot a woman to death then took aim at Ranger Gillingham who responded to the sound of gunfire. With little regard for his own safety, Gillingham rushed the shooter, a troubled 19-year-old, and tackled him. The killer did have time to get off a couple of shots at the Ranger, narrowly missing him.

Gillingham had the fight of his life on his hands as the scrappy youngster fought like a wounded bear. Finally, Gillingham subdued the murderer with a crashing blow from his right fist and handcuffed him.

Gillingham's bare-fisted charge at the rifle-wielding killer could have ended much differently. Ranger # 103 George Pauls remembers training with Gillingham and that he was a crack shot with his revolver. No doubt Gillingham could have killed the accused in question, but instead he tackled the man and thus brought him to justice.

Men like John Hogan and Bruce Gillingham ensured that the Rangers earned a lofty place in the history of Newfoundland. But it is also for their regular day-to-day duties and constant courtesy that the Rangers earned a place in the hearts of Newfoundlanders.

References

1. Crane, Norman. "Address to the Newfoundland Historical Society" March 25, 1982.
2. Goodyear, Cyril. "The Road to Nowhere." Creative Publishers: St. John's.
3. Horwood, Harold. "History of the Newfoundland Ranger Force." Breakwater, St. John's.
4. McGrath, Darrin. "The Law of the Land", in The Downhomer Magazine, September 2005.
5. McGrath, Darrin. "Window on Yesterday," in The Telegram September 10, 2005 page B-1.
6. Parsons, Ches. Research notes and personal stories of the Newfoundland Rangers.

7. Pauls, George. Notes on the Rangers.
8. Pilgrim, Earl. "Will Anyone Search for Danny?" Creative Publishers, St. John's.
9. Smith, Robert. Research notes and personal stories of the Newfoundland Rangers.

~ Chapter Three ~

RANGER BIOGRAPHIES

The American sociologist C. Wright Mills postulated that the proper focus of any social scientific study should be to investigate the juncture between biography and history. Each individual has a biography or life story. But that life story is played out within a given historical time-frame and so history influences and shapes biography. The small-scale, life-story of a person is situated within the broad sweep of history.

But of course, biography also has an impact on history. The lives of men and women can shape and influence and change the sweep of events. Key figures come onto the stage at critical junctures; for example Winston Churchill in Britain during WWII.

The well-known criminologist Elliot Leyton has made use of the life story in many of his books. In the best selling work Hunting Humans Leyton delves into the gruesome biographies of mass murderers and serial killers.

Likewise, in Dying Hard Leyton examines the life stories of hard-rock miners from the Burin Peninsula who contracted silicosis while drilling in fluorspar mines in St. Lawrence.

In both books, Leyton's use of biography helps illuminate two types of violence; murder and industrial carnage.

What follows in this book are short biographic sketches of the 204 enlisted men who served in the Newfoundland Rangers. Clearly, their life stories were profoundly shaped by the historical period in which they lived. It was the "dirty thirties" and self-government had fallen when the Rangers went into the field. Unemployment and poverty raged through much of outport Newfoundland. But by 1939 the world was at war and those events too had a crucial impact on the Rangers.

At the same time, the life stories of the Rangers had an impact on Newfoundland history. For example, the work of the Rangers helped facilitate the survival and functioning of the Commission of Government. Likewise, the Rangers helped ease the troubles and burdens of many outport Newfoundlanders whom they served.

After the Rangers were absorbed into the RCMP in 1950, many ex-Rangers went on to lead successful professional lives which continued to shape events in Newfoundland history.

It is hoped that the following biographical sketches will not only commemorate the work of the individuals who served as Rangers, but will also help facilitate a broader understanding of the Ranger Force and its impacts on Newfoundland history.

Regimental Number 1 - Brian White

#1

Brian White holds the honor of being the first man to enlist in the Newfoundland Ranger Force. He was sworn in on July 9, 1935.

Brian was born on March 7, 1910, in St. George's, Newfoundland. His father Matthew worked with the Reid Newfoundland Railway Company and his mother Christine (Maher) looked after the home.

Brian earned his grade eleven from St. Bonaventure's College in St. John's where he excelled in both academics and athletics. Then he joined the Newfoundland Constabulary. This makes him one of 22 men who transferred from the Constabulary to the Rangers.

Brian met his future wife, May Wylan, in 1934. May was a widow with a 13-year old daughter, Bernice, who went on to become a civilian employee of the Ranger Force. In fact, her name appears on the plaque commemorating the Rangers on the grounds of the Colonial Building in St. John's.

May and Brian married on October 15, 1936, and they had a daughter of their own, Christine. She was very helpful in providing photos of her father and biographical information. Christine O'Halleran resides in Ontario today.

Brian Kennedy of St. John's is named for Brian White. Kennedy's father, Edward F. Kennedy, and Brian White were best friends. They attended school together at St. Bon's and played on the Boyle trophy-winning hockey team there. Edward Kennedy thought so highly of Brian White that he named his son after him.

White's namesake, Brian Kennedy, describes Brian White as a "prince of a man." He goes on to say that White was a great athlete and a dedicated family man.

After leaving the Ranger Force, Brian White studied law and joined the Magistracy. He later became the head of the Newfoundland Liquor Commission.

#2

Regimental Number 2 - Leslie O'Reilly

Leslie O'Reilly was born in St. John's on June 4, 1913, to Margaret (Fleming) and Patrick O'Reilly, a farmer on Long Pond Road. Patrick was also employed as a journalist with the Evening Telegram.

Leslie graduated with grade eleven from St. Bon's College and distinguished himself as an outstanding athlete in hockey and track and field. Like Brian White, Ranger # 1, Leslie was a member of many hockey teams that won the famous Boyle Trophy and was number four oar on the St. Bon's rowing team.

After joining the first draft of the Rangers, Leslie was posted to Badger, a booming logging town in central Newfoundland. Leslie spoke highly of the family he boarded with in Badger and also spoke of how difficult traveling was in those days.

While stationed in Badger he met and married Grace Glover. The couple has two daughters, Irene, a nurse, and Beverley, a teacher.

Leslie was later posted to Deer Lake, another logging town, and left the Rangers to join the woods staff of Bowaters Paper Company. He retired from Bowaters in June 1979 at which time he was Division Accountant with the Woods Department at the company's operation in Corner Brook.

During his retirement he walked daily, skied, skated and gardened as the seasons dictated. He lived in Corner Brook until his death in November 1994.

His daughter Beverly was a great help in putting this account together. Leslie's brother-in-law, Reg Mercer, was also a Ranger.

#3

Regimental Number 3 - Edward English

Edward English was born on October 23, 1908. He had two brothers, Jack and Dermot, and his father was Captain Edward English, Harbour Master of St. John's, while his mom Kathleen O'Driscoll was a Registered Nurse.

Like Rangers # 1 and 2, Edward went to school at St. Bon's College where he completed high school. His daughter Kathleen (Nickerson) believes that her father went to sea before joining the Rangers because of the family's close association with sailing. His father was a sea-going skipper, while his brother Dermot had command of the HMCS Vallyfield in May 1944 when it was sunk by a U-boat off the coast of Newfoundland. All 125 men on board were lost.

Edward joined the Rangers in 1935 and was stationed to Hebron, Labrador. However, he wintered at Nain with Ranger Frank Mercer until they built the detachment in Hebron in 1936. Resident Missionary George Harp also helped with the construction.

The adventure that being a Ranger promised helped lure him into service, but his daughter says the fact it "was a good job" also attracted the youthful Edward.

On July 13, 1939, Edward married registered nurse Gertrude Harvey of Harbour Breton. The couple were wed for 53 years before Edward passed away. Gertrude left this world on July 17, 2001. The couple had one child, Kathleen Loretta.

After he left the Rangers, Edward worked as head of Maintenance at the U.S. Base Fort Pepperell, in St. John's. The family then moved to Quebec and Ontario, where they owned a farm and a grocery store respectively. Later in life, Edward worked as director of warehousing for General Electric Company in Ontario. The couple retired to Trenton, Ontario

Kathleen recalls some stories her father used to tell. One, also told by Norman Crane, is that while in Hebron English accompanied Ranger Frank Mercer to arrest Esau Gillingham for murder. While traveling by dog team a snow storm came on and Mercer and English became separated. They arrived back at the detachment a day apart.

Edward also spoke a lot about the Inuit (at the time called Eskimos) in Labrador, and of time spent patrolling the coast in a boat with his wife. Together they did everything from pulling teeth to delivering babies.

Regimental Number 4 - Harold Smith

#4

Harold Smith was born in Twillingate on March 8, 1912, to Agnes Smith and Cecil V. Smith. Cecil was a medical doctor, while Agnes looked after the home and children.

Young Harold matriculated from Bishop Feild school in St. John's. After leaving school he joined the Ranger Force in July 1935 and remained in the force until January 1938. During that time he was stationed in Lewisporte, Gambo and Springdale.

Harold says that he joined the Rangers because he was the "outdoors type" and the work appealed to him. He recalls that Ranger training was a great experience characterized by happy times and fellowship amongst the recruits.

One very memorable experience that stands out in Harold's mind of his Ranger service involved a strike by Bowater Company loggers in the towns of Robert's and Tommie's Arms.

Smith was dispatched to the scene where he found disgruntled loggers demanding a meeting with senior company management. Smith contacted the company who sent some managers via coastal steamer to meet with the loggers. However, Smith also called in reinforcements, and the Head Ranger, Major Anderson, and a squad of twenty Constabulary officers arrived to keep order amongst the unruly loggers.

After leaving the Rangers in 1938, Harold was appointed Chief of the Forest Fire Protection Service with the Forestry Branch of the Department of Natural Resources. On June 28, 1943, he signed on with the Canadian Navy and served overseas. Honorably discharged in 1945, he returned to work as chief forest fire warden, where he remained until December 31, 1950. At that time he transferred to the Federal Department of Fisheries and Oceans where he remained as Chief of the Protection Branch until his retirement in 1976.

In 1953, Harold married Dorothy Inkpen and they raised two daughters, Lynda (Tock) and Lois (Aubut).

Regimental Number 5 - Frederick Beauchamp

#5

Fred Beauchamp was born in Recontre West on November 10, 1910. His father James was a blacksmith and his mother Louisa (Durnford) was a seamstress. The family moved to Port aux Basques where his father continued this trade by opening his own smithy.

After completing high school, Fred went to work as a fisheries officer and joined the Rangers in July 1935 as a career choice. While in Whitbourne he attained the rank of Sergeant and was later stationed at Grand Bank and Twillingate.

In 1938, he married Lillian Tavernor and they had one son, Robert. Fred served in the Rangers for almost eight years. He left the force in 1943, a decision he made following the loss of his wife's father and two brothers in the sinking of the SS Caribou.

After leaving the Rangers he was employed at the U.S. Base in Stephenville. Later, he returned to Port aux Basques where he owned and operated a very successful hardware and furniture store.

Regimental Number 6 - Charles Summers

Charles L. K. Summers was born on January 5, 1910, in St. John's. He passed peacefully away in 1999 in St. Catharine's, Ontario.

Charles attended school in St. John's. After joining the Rangers in 1935, he was stationed in Twillingate, Goose Bay and Cartwright.

He married Isobel Smith from Heart's Content on September 5, 1939, and the couple had three daughters, two of whom were born in Cartwright; Joan (Allan) and Patricia (Makinson).

Charles left the Rangers after five years' service and moved to Ontario in 1945. The following year

#6

he and his wife had another daughter, Kathy (Picken), who lives in Victoria, British Columbia, and is a museum curator.

Prior to retirement, Charles was employed with Canadian Immigration at the Canada-U.S. border.

Charles and his wife lived in a suburb of St. Catharine's, Ontario, called Port Dalhousie. Isobel died in 1994, and Charles died five years later at the age of 89.

Regimental Number 7 - Leslie Chaffey

Born in St. John's on October 2, 1910, Leslie "Les" Chaffey was the son of grocers James and Ada Chaffey. Les completed grade eleven at Bishop Feild College and prior to joining the Rangers worked as a clerk in his family's grocery store.

After joining the Rangers in 1935, Les was sent to Labrador. In fact, in a letter written in April 1993, he recalled that he was the first Ranger to reach the big land. Les arrived in Battle Harbour aboard the SS Kyle in the latter part of October 1935. Two years of supplies and construction

#7

materials to build a detachment post were also off-loaded and stored in one of Baine Johnston's buildings. Charlie Hoff, manager of Baine Johnston's, put the young Ranger up for the night. Later he boarded with Charlie and Mollie Mangrove. George Smith of Battle Harbour was a great help to the young Ranger and used his sled and dog-team to transport him about on patrols.

He was stationed at Battle Harbour but the district included Spear Harbour, Fox Harbour, Lewis Bay, Mary's Harbour, Cape Charles, Henley

Harbour and Green Bay. In 1936 he was transferred to Forteau, on the Labrador Straits. Les recalled the trouble experienced in helping the mentally ill get any help on this isolated coast.

Les married Mary (Russell) in St. Peter's Anglican Church in Forteau on May 24, 1937. The couple has one child, Leslie Patricia, who goes by the name "Pat."

Les left the Rangers in August 1937. He managed a trading store for Baine Johnston's in Battle Harbour and later he and his wife went to work for the Grenfell mission in Mary's Harbour, Labrador. Mary worked as a nurse and Les looked after the outside work. In October 1939 the couple learned that Mary's mother was very ill so they moved to Philippi, West Virginia.

While there, Les completed training in X-ray technology at Alderson-Broaddus College. He then worked as an X-ray technician at the Myers Clinic Hospital until 1978 when he retired after 51 years of service.

Les was a deeply spiritual man and was ordained as a deacon in St. Paul's Episcopal Church in Philippi in 1964. In 1965 he was made a priest and served as rector of both St. Paul's and St. Matthias Episcopal Churches.

Les passed away on April 15, 1996. His wife died on January 26, 2001.

Regimental Number 8 - David Morgan

#8

Born in St. John's on May 28, 1911, David Morgan was the son of Abraham and Emma (nee Boone). After completing grade eleven in St. John's, David was employed as a carpenter with Carnell's Funeral Home. He joined the Rangers in July 1935 and was a member of the first contingent.

David was stationed at North West River, Labrador. He would later tell his family that he had to build a detachment to live in and spent a miserable winter there where he almost froze to death.

He was later stationed in Marystown on the Burin Peninsula, where he served in 1937. It is thought that he left the Rangers by the end of 1938 as his name is no longer on personnel lists at that time.

David married Maggie "Jean" Smith on June 27, 1939, and they had seven children: Gerald, who died in infancy; David; Sandra; Wayne; Wanda; Gary; and Arthur.

After leaving the Rangers, David worked as a time-keeper at Browning

Harvey Factory in St. John's, but he took up work at the U.S. base Fort Pepperrell when it opened in 1941. He transferred to the U.S. airbase in Stephenville, Harmon Field, in 1942, where he worked as a first aid person.

Regimental Number 9 - Joseph Delahunty

#9

Joseph Delahunty was born in Calvert on the Southern Shore on the 5th of February 1907. His parents were Richard and Margaret (nee Power).

Joseph attended school in Calvert where he earned grade eleven. After completing high school he joined the ranks of the Newfoundland Constabulary. But in 1935 the promise of adventure and better pay lured him into the Rangers. He was later posted at Twillingate, Burin and St. Anthony. His brother Michael Ranger # 40.

Joseph recalled with fondness his training at Whitbourne and the close friendships forged with the townspeople there and in nearby Colinet.

In August 1937, he married M. DeSales Goff and the couple had eleven children: Richard, Mary, Paula, Margaret, Kathryn, Brian, Claire, Carmel, Josephine, John and Brenda.

After six years of Ranger service, he left the Force in August 1941 and settled in his native Calvert. He first went fishing for a living and later operated a fish plant which sold its product to Harvey and Company in St. John's. Later he got out of the fish business and operated a convenience store and gas bar.

Regimental Number 10 - Edward Martin

#10

Edward Martin was the son of a cooper or barrel-maker. He was born in St. John's and was educated at the Methodist Academy where he earned grade eleven. He rose through the ranks of the Ranger Force to become Chief Ranger.

Edward had a variety of jobs before he joined the Rangers. In 1927 he worked with Ayre and Sons in the hardware department. In 1929 he worked as a driller at the Buchans Mine, and in 1932 he joined the Newfoundland Constabulary, where he lived in the barracks and earned $50 per month. He served three years with the Constabulary before signing on with the Rangers because of the more varied work it promised.

Within a year of joining the Rangers he was made a Sergeant and Section Non-Commissioned Officer (NCO) for Labrador. He married Emily Wier in 1944. The couple had two children, a son and a daughter, born in Halifax and St. John's respectively.

Edward served 15 years as a Ranger and saw postings in Whitbourne, Cartwright and Bonne Bay. During his tenure as a Ranger, he rose through the ranks to earn the title of Chief Ranger.

After the Rangers were decommissioned in 1950, Martin joined the RCMP and earned the rank of Assistant Commissioner. After retiring from the Mounties in 1969 he settled in Regina, Sask.

He also became a Judge and following that was National Director of the Corps of Commissionaires.

Regimental Number 11 - Thomas Curnew

#11

Thomas "Tom" Curnew was born in Belloram on April 7, 1909, to Frederick, a teacher/customs officer, and Caroline (nee West). Tom received his early education in his home town and later attended King's College in Winsor, Nova Scotia.

After finishing college, Tom worked for the Bank of Nova Scotia in Sydney, Nova Scotia. Later he joined the Newfoundland Constabulary. Eventually, in 1935 he joined the ranks of the Rangers.

The excitement of being part of a new force with varied, challenging responsibilities attracted the twenty-six year old to sign on. For ten years he served as a Ranger in places such as La Scie, Burin, St. Anthony, Rose Blanche and Port aux Basques.

In October 1939, while stationed in St. Anthony, he married Marion Mildred Penney, the daughter of Edgar and Annie (nee Green) Penny. They had one son, Gerry, who was born in the Burgeo Cottage Hospital.

When Tom Curnew got word that he was to be posted to Nain, Labrador, Mildred put her foot down. She had grown up in St. Anthony and had enough of the north. She encouraged Tom to leave the Rangers and take employment with Bowaters in Corner Brook.

Upon leaving the Ranger Force in 1945, Tom Curnew accepted employment as an accountant with Bowaters Pulp and Paper Company in Corner Brook, where he worked until his retirement in 1986. He later relocated to St. John's to be closer to Gerry and his wife Bertha and their sons Stephen, Garry and David. Tom lived with Gerry and Bertha for the last nine years of his life. He passed away in 1994.

Gerry Curnew remembers his father talking about traveling by dog sled over the ice in a snowstorm. When the dogs would venture near the edge of the ice and you could hear the sea running, the team would then instinctively strike back for land.

In another case, Tom spent seven days and nights guarding an American military plane that had crashed near Port aux Basques. It was feared German spies might try to survey the wreckage for secrets.

He also recalled one story in which he had a great meal with people along the west coast of the Northern Peninsula. Desert was a dish of bakeapples. Only after the meal was eaten did the lady of the house reveal she had shucked the bakeapples by sucking on them! Tom Curnew refused to eat bakeapples for the rest of his life unless he knew the person who was giving the berries to him.

Tom Curnew was an avid amateur photographer and he took hundreds of photos while he was a Ranger. Gerry discovered the negatives in a trunk after his father's death and today is proud to own a vast collection of pictures depicting life in outport Newfoundland during the 1930's.

Tom passed away on June 3, 1994, at age 85. He was very active up to the last year of his life and was proud of his Ranger service.

Regimental Number 12 - John Nichols

#12

You might say John Nichols had an eye for fine things. After leaving the Newfoundland Rangers he studied optometry.

Brooklyn, Bonavista Bay was home for Ranger John Nichols. He was born March 27, 1912, and attended school in Brooklyn and later at Bishop Feild College in St. John's, where he earned grade eleven. His father was the first Rector of St. Michael's Anglican Church on Casey Street.

Prior to signing on with the Rangers, John worked as a clerk with Job Brothers in St John's. The Ranger Force promised a vastly different lifestyle for the merchant's clerk and so he joined up in 1935. He often talked of the training received at Whitbourne under Major Stick and Staff Sgt. Anderton.

Over the course of five years he served in the following communities: Port Saunders; Bonne Bay, Springdale, Marystown and NorthWest River, Labrador.

In October 1940 he left the Rangers to join the Royal Canadian Air

Force which he served until the end of the war in 1945.

In July 1945, he married Peggy Kirkcacdy in Fifeshire, Scotland, and together they had four children: Anne (Averiss); Katherine (Shears); Robert; Angus. Later in life he married for the second time, wedding Marie Butt.

After leaving the RCAF, John studied optometry in London, England. He practiced optometry in Newfoundland from 1950 until his retirement in 1984. He lived to the fine age of 92 and passed away in January 2005.

Regimental Number 13 - Jack Thomas

Jack Thomas was born on September 22, 1911, and died May 1, 1965. His father John was from Wales, while his mother Charlotte (Carberry) was from St. John's.

Jack earned grade eleven and in 1935 joined the first draft of Rangers. He trained at Whitbourne and was later posted to Englee, La Scie, Port aux Basques and Harbour Breton.

He married schoolteacher Dulcie Carew of Port aux Basques on December 31, 1941, and they had three children; Deanne (Peters). Doris (Blackwood), and Trevor.

Deanne says her dad was an avid photographer. "My dad was always taking pictures which at one time he used to develop himself. He used to use a strong attached to the shutter to take family portraits of all of us. If you look closely you can sometimes see the string in his pictures."

Deanne's own love of photography began at an early age when she borrowed her father's camera to take pictures of her younger siblings.

Jack remained with the Ranger Force for ten years and after leaving the force settled in St. John's where he worked as a salesman with Browning Harvey Ltd.

#14

Regimental Number 14 - Danny Corcoran

Sadly, Danny Corcoran is perhaps one of the best known Rangers. His recognition comes from the fact that he got lost while on patrol on the rugged Northern Peninsula in March 1936 and perished from frostbite related injuries. Corcoran's tale is the focus of Earl Pilgrim's 1986 book Will Anyone Search for Danny? Corcoran's story is also told in Harold Horwood's 1986 History of the Newfoundland Ranger Force.

Danny Corcoran was one of the first thirty Rangers who trained at Whitbourne in the summer of 1935. In the autumn, he went north on the SS Prospero to his posting in the isolated settlement of Harbour Deep.

Danny grew up in St. John's and was a member of the hiking club in which forty-mile cross country hikes were commonly organized and carried out. In March 1936, Danny received reports of caribou being poached in large numbers so he decided to patrol across the width of the Northern Peninsula and meet Ranger # 12 John Nicols. Unfortunately, Danny fell into a brook, lost much of his gear and was unable to light a fire. He almost got back to Harbour Deep, but due to a weakened state was unable to make it.

He survived for almost twenty days with frozen feet and hands. When finally found by a search party he was unable to crawl and was lying in a pool of water. The search party from Englee took him on dogsled to White Bay. From there, he was taken by the United Church clergyman's boat to St. Anthony hospital. The journey took seven agonizing days and Danny succumbed to his injuries while in hospital on April 7, 1936.

Danny Corcoran was buried in Mount Carmel Cemetery, St. John's.

Regimental Number 15 - Clarence Dwyer

#15

Clarence "Clar" Dwyer was born in Harbour Grace, March 5, 1910. His father Alexander was a member of the Newfoundland Constabulary, while his mother Louise (nee Hodder) was a housewife.

After finishing grade eleven he worked with an American auto firm. In 1935, he took the big step of joining the Newfoundland Rangers on the advice of his father. He was posted to Glenwood, Harbour Deep, Jackson's Arm, Port Hope Simpson, Forteau, Norris Arm and Lewisporte. On March 2, 1942, while stationed in Forteau, Labrador, Clar was crossing the Straits in a small boat when he encountered a number of submarines but they gave him no trouble. However, on August 4, the American transport Chatham was sunk and he had to arrange for food, clothing and shelter for 87 survivors for five days before they were moved out of the community. He was personally left short of food and clothing but not unmindful of the tragedy of war.

In 1940, he wed Lucie Janes and they had a large family: Frederick; Gerald; June; Cynthia; Eric; David; Lloyd; Pamela.

Clar remained with the Rangers until 1950 at which time he joined the ranks of the RCMP. He retired to pension from the RCMP and later settled in St. John's. He passed away on August 29, 1993.

#16

Regimental Number 16 - Edward Delaney

Edward Delaney grew up in beautiful Bay Roberts. His father Patrick was involved in the family fishing industry and died at an early age. His mother, Ita (nee Burke), was a well-educated lady and worked as a schoolteacher.

Like his mom, Edward went on to be highly educated for the time and it is thought he earned his grade eleven from St. Bon's. Before entering the Rangers, Edward was employed as a schoolteacher and reportedly taught for three years on the French islands of St. Pierre and Miquelon.

He joined the Rangers on July 18, 1935, and was engaged with the rank of Sergeant-in- charge of Quartermaster Stores in Whitbourne and Kilbride. He stayed with the Rangers for the entire time the force existed, 15 years and two weeks.

In July 1950, when the Rangers were absorbed into the RCMP, Edward transferred to the Mounted Police. He did well in the RCMP and earned the rank of Sergeant Major, the highest Non-Commissioned Officers rank in the provinces being policed by the RCMP. He was honorably discharged from the RCMP after 35 years of service and settled in St. John's with his wife Helen (Godden). He passed away on September 2, 1972, while watching the famous Canada-Russia hockey game.

Delaney is remembered as the author of Ranger Force "Epistles." These stories were laced with wit, humour and sarcasm about Rangers' shortcomings.

Regimental Number 17 - Clarence Robertson

Clarence (Ginger) Robertson grew up in the capital city of St. John's where he was born on March 1914. His parents were William and Sarah.

We were unable to determine precisely where he attended school but he undoubtedly had earned grade eleven as this was required for entry into the Ranger Force.

It is known that from August 23, 1933, to July 19, 1935, he was a member of the Newfoundland Constabulary. He joined the Rangers in 1935.

Clarence was stationed at Deer Lake in January 1936, but it is not known how long he remained with the Rangers.

It is known that he joined the Royal Air Force when hostilities broke out between Germany and the United Kingdom. Robertson graduated as a navigator and later earned the rank of Flying Officer, service number 53021.

One of his tours was flying with Coastal Command to Iceland as a member of 512 Squadron. When the first aircraft of the RAF Ferry Command left Gander for England, Clarence (Ginger) Robertson was the navigator on board.

On March 21, 1944, he was serving with the RAF when his plane crashed and he was killed at the untimely age of 30. He is buried in Brookfield Military Cemetery, United Kingdom.

Regimental Number 18 - John Selby Brown

John Brown was born in St. John's on December 29, 1912. His father Thomas was a ship owner and carpenter. His mother Rachel Mercer looked after the home. In 1919, the family moved to Brooklyn, New York, but returned to St. John's in 1932.

John was now twenty and had completed grade eleven. He joined the Newfoundland Constabulary in 1932. In 1935 he left the Constabulary to join the Newfoundland Rangers. His brother Eric later joined the Rangers (# 36).

#18

In 1938, he wed Elva Hopkins and they had one child, Ruth. He served as a Ranger for five years and was posted to detachments in St. Anthony, Twillingate, Harbour Breton, Englee, Forteau and Port Saunders. It is thought he enlisted in the Canadian Army during the Second World War. He passed away on November 13, 1943, after a brief battle with cancer.

John Brown kept a diary during his years as a Ranger and in 1973 these were published by Elva Stuckless (his wife) under the title "The Writings of Ranger J.S. Brown."

The introduction to the book is written by his daughter Ruth. In addition to recollecting his time as a Ranger there are also some poems that Brown wrote including one titled "Fisherman's Wife:"

> Out o'er the sea the storm descends
> While in prayer and sleep my tired head bends;
> But sleep I can't, and I pray I must,
> A prayer of faith, of hope and trust.
>
> For a small craft rides on the angry deep,
> As I my lonely vigil keep;
> So sleep I can't and pray I must
> A fervent prayer or hope and trust

Regimental Number 19 - Frederick Noseworthy

#19

Frederick (Fred) Noseworthy was born in 1907, the fifth of nine children, the eldest of Lorenzo and Mary Olivia's three sons. Lorenzo was from Bryant's Cove, while Mary was from Port de Gave, but the couple raised their family in Spaniard's Bay.

According to Fred's nephew, retired Colonel Frederick Noseworthy, the family was well off at a time when many Newfoundlanders had desolate hardship. Lorenzo ran a successful business as a merchant and schooner owner. The family lived in a large Victorian home adjacent to their general store in Spaniard's Bay.

They were staunch Anglicans and all the children were sent to private schools for their post secondary education. Fred attended Bishop Feild College for his advanced education.

As the eldest male Fred was apprenticed to his father and made many offshore voyages aboard family schooners. He made at least one trip to "the Labrador" with Skipper Bob Bartlett of nearby Brigus.

While he was a student at Bishop Feild, one of his father's ships, the Una, drew into St. John's harbour and Fred decided to catch a ride back home to Spaniard's Bay. The journey, however, almost cost him his life. The Una ran into a gale and was wrecked. Fred helped lower a dory from the foundering ship and helped save the crew and a disabled person on board. All hands managed to make shore safely somewhere north of Carbonear.

The wreck of the Una is thought to have played a large role in Fred's decision to enter the Rangers as the loss of the vessel near bankrupted the Noseworthy family. Lorenzo died in 1931 and within three years the Noseworthys were out of business.

Fred would have been looking for a job at the time the Rangers were recruiting. According to his nephew, "fate put him in a Ranger uniform instead of a suit."

Fred was mature, strong willed, physically fit, well educated and loyal. According to his nephew, he cared for others, had a spirit for adventure and was resourceful. His younger brother, Eric (# 65), followed him into the Rangers a few years after he joined.

Sadly, Fred and his wife both developed tuberculosis in 1942 and died without having had any children.

Regimental Number 20 - Vince Nugent

Vince Nugent was born in Kelligrews in July 1904. His father Michael was a caretaker for Bowring Park, while his mother Sarah (nee Purcell) looked after the home.

After completing grade eleven, young Vince went to the United States in search of work. He was employed working with a railroad company. However, the adventure and promise of good pay and benefits drew him back to Newfoundland and the Ranger Force.

He joined the Rangers in July 1935 and was stationed at St. Alban's and Bonne Bay. He stayed

#20

with the Rangers for about three years and attained the rank of Corporal.

He married Catherine Duff sometime after leaving the Rangers and together they had six children; Magdalen; Vincent; Desmond; Patricia; Delores; Rose.

After leaving the Rangers, he was employed with Posts and Telegraphs in St. John's. He also was the Post Master at Argentia. But he later returned to the United States and was employed as a Telegraph Operator in New Haven, Conn. He eventually retired and settled in Corner Brook.

Regimental Number 21 - Val Duff

Val Duff was born in St. John's in February 1916 at 72 Monroe Street. His father Edward Duff was a master cooper and later a farmer, while his mother Elizabeth Walsh was a homemaker.

Val attended Holy Cross School where he earned grade eleven. After leaving school he worked in the cooperage with his father. However, Val sought a more adventuresome life and so he joined the Rangers and was stationed at detachments in St. Lawrence, Harbour Deep and Labrador.

#21

A characteristic of Val that made him well suited for work with the Rangers was his love of the woods and nature. He thoroughly enjoyed fishing and hunting and was at ease when traveling in the country. He instinctively knew his way around the woods and always returned on the same route and never got lost while traveling in the back country.

Val married Anne Maher in the late 1930s and they had six children: Val, Patsy, David, Robert, Maureen, and Brenda.

After leaving the Rangers, Val started a grocery business, Spot Cash Grocery, at the corner of Flower's Hill and Monroe Street in St. John's. He was a good businessman and was very successful. True to his boyhood roots, when not working he spent his spare time hunting and fishing.

Regimental Number 22 - Alan Legrow

Alan Legrow would eventually become a Provincial Court Judge. It was a long way to the Bench from his humble beginnings in Broad Cove, Bay de Verde, in October 1914.

His father, Thomas, was a welfare officer while his mother, Daisy, looked after the home and children. Alan attended Salem School in Broad Cove, and later Prince of Wales College in St. John's where he earned grade eleven.

After completing school he joined the ranks of the Newfoundland Constabulary where he served for many years. He joined the Rangers in 1935 and was stationed at Whitbourne, Springdale, Deer Lake, St. George's, Port aux Basques and Grand Bank.

On August 22, 1938, he married Jennie Butler and they had three children: Marilyn; Robert and Bruce.

In 1950, when the RCMP replaced the Rangers, Alan joined that police force and was the only member of the Rangers to keep his rank of Sergeant. After retiring from the RCMP, he was appointed a Provincial Court Judge.

His son, Bruce, served as a Provincial Court Judge during part of his father's bench service. Their concurrent service is believed to be the only "father and son" judicial service at the same time in Newfoundland history.

In 1986, he married Ruth Alcock.

Regimental Number 23 - Harold Guzzwell

Harold Guzzwell was born in St. John's on May 15, 1915. His mother, Annie (Edgecombe), was a homemaker, while his father Ernest operated a horse drawn cab and a farm on Logy Bay Road, St. John's.

Harold attended Centenary Hall School in the capital city where he completed high school. In 1934-35, Harold was a member of the mounted police unit with the Newfoundland Constabulary. After joining the Rangers in 1935 for the adventure of it, he was posted to detachments in Hopedale, Port Saunders, Bonne Bay and Point Leamington. Harold served for five years with the Rangers and went overseas during WWII as a gunner in the Royal Artillery. His brother Gladstone also joined the Rangers (# 41).

Upon returning from military service, Harold started farming at Cormack on the island's west coast. On May 17, 1947, he married Mary Green of Winterton. Due to health reasons, Harold later took a job administering the Veteran's Land Act after which he resided in Corner Brook.

A memorable Ranger experience for Harold occurred in 1939 when he served as part of the honour guard when the King of England visited Newfoundland. He was stationed in Port Saunders at the time and had to walk to Deer Lake in order to catch the train for St. John's. On his walk he spent a night at the home of Mrs. Georgina Payne of Cow Head. Mrs. Payne told Harold's younger brother Fred the story some years later.

Regimental Number 24 - Gordon Fitzpatrick

Born in Marystown on September 4, 1916, Gordon Fitzpatrick was the son of a Customs Officer. Gordon earned his grade eleven in Marystown. Prior to joining the Rangers, he worked with the Fire Department in St. John's from 1933 to 1935.

#24

Gordon joined the Rangers in 1935 for the challenges it presented. He served for fifteen years until the force was absorbed into the RCMP after Confederation. Gordon rose to the rank of Sgt. Major.

As a Ranger, he was stationed at many detachments including Cartwright (1935), Stephenville Crossing, Bonne Bay (1947), Bay L'Argent, St. Lawrence and St George's (1950).

He married Sarah Gallant in August 1943. The couple had five children: Genevieve, Donald, Robert, Kathleen and Michael.

In 1950, he became a Mountie. Upon retirement from that force as a Sgt. Major, he was employed by the Roman Catholic School Board up until he retired for a second time.

In civilian life he served as Executive Secretary of the Federation of School Boards for the province. He passed away on April 19, 1973.

His brother Tom was Ranger # 127.

#25

Regimental Number 25 - Frank Mercer

Frank Mercer was born in Bay Roberts on August 2, 1914. His father Bethlehem - "Beth" - was a school teacher and later a telegraph operator with the Bay Roberts Branch of the Western Union Cable Company. His mother Sophie (Mercer) was a homemaker who looked after the family.

Frank was highly educated and had earned grade eleven at Bay Roberts Anglican Academy as well as a teaching certificate from Memorial University College on Parade Street in St. John's.

But, instead of going teaching, Frank joined the Newfoundland Constabulary. In 1934, he was one of the first squad of ten Constabulary officers to be stationed in Labrador, at Hebron.

After becoming Ranger Number 25, Frank served for fifteen years and two weeks, the life of the Force. He was posted to several Labrador detachments including Nain, Hebron and Cartwright. On the island, he saw action at Marystown, Rose Blanche, Bay L'Argent, Deer Lake and Twillingate.

In a letter to the authors, Frank said that he joined the Rangers for "better training, better pay, and better living conditions." He also highlights the Ranger training as a memorable experience because the "Rangers were modeled after the RCMP and were trained by that force."

In 1943, Frank wed Ada Rebecca Goosney of Deer Lake. The two were joined in matrimony in Corner Brook. They had four children; twins Frank Jr. and Gordon; Barry and Diane.

While a Ranger, Frank had many exciting experiences. One in particular was his trek in 1936 when he traveled from Okak, north of Nain, to Cartwright and back, a distance of 1,400 miles by dog sled. The trip, which took over two months, was for the purpose of delivering a dead Inuit, Mark Kennitok, to Cartwright for an autopsy in order to determine whether or not trapper Esau Gillingham was guilty of his murder. It turned out no murder had been committed. Kennitok died of alcohol abuse.

In 1938, while stationed in Hebron, 22-year-old Mercer had to deal with the reversion of a number of Inuit to heathensim. An Inuit named Rosa Tuglavina, who had a mental condition, gave birth to a child. The medicine man, Jefta, said the child should be sacrificed in order for Rosa to regain her health. Mercer subsequently took the baby to the Ranger detachment. He then arrested able bodied men, including Jefta, and moved them to a distant encampment with enough food to last until spring. He also shot their dogs. As Mercer stated, "harsh treatment, perhaps, but necessary in a harsh land."

Frank said in his letter to the authors that "with Confederation, the Ranger Force was integrated with the Royal Canadian Mounted Police. My official number with this force was 16168. Following retirement from this force, I settled in Bay Roberts, my hometown."

Before he retired from the RCMP, Staff Sgt. Mercer served as the Labrador Section Non-Commissioned Officer based in Goose Bay. Thus, he became the only person known to have served in Labrador with three different law enforcement agencies.

After retiring from the RCMP in 1969, Mercer was appointed as provincial government commissioner for Labrador. His law enforcement service in the "Big Land" had prepared him well for this post.

He served as commissioner until 1976 at which time he and his wife, Ada, retired to Bay Roberts where he named their home Labrador House.

In 2003 Frank was the subject of a book *Probably Without Equal* written by John Parsons.

Frank Mercer passed away at Carbonear Hospital on October 10, 2005, at age 91.

Regimental Number 26 - Morris Christian

#26

Morris Christian was born in Trinity, Trinity Bay. After completing grade eleven, he articled as an accountant with a Newfoundland firm. However, the adventure promised by becoming a Ranger lured him away from his balance sheets and he joined the Rangers in July 1935.

Morris was posted to various detachments including Rose Blanche, Nain, Battle Harbour and St. Anthony.

Along the way at these various communities he met and married a nurse, Emma Grimes. They had one child, Denny Christian.

After leaving the Rangers, Morris became the manager of a car dealership in the central Newfoundland community of Grand Falls.

Morris Christian had many exciting adventures during his time as a Ranger. In November 1947, he helped rescue the crew of the SS Langleecraq, a 5,000 tonne British freighter which ran aground near St. Anthony on the Northern Peninsula. Two members of the crew were lost but Christian organized rescue operations which saved the remaining 41. In another of his adventures, he had to eat his sled dogs to survive on a patrol to the Churchill Falls area in Labrador. Morris also crossed the

Strait of Belle Isle from Battle Harbour to St. Anthony in a snowstorm to deal with an unruly individual in St. Anthony. No doubt, Morris got the adventure he sought when he originally signed on as a Ranger.

#27

Regimental Number 27 - Ronald Peet

Ronald (Ron) Peet was born on October 16, 1913, and passed away on May 22, 2002. He was laid to rest from the Chapel of Barrett's Funeral Home in St. John's on May 25, 2002.

Ron was born in Sydney Mines, Cape Breton. His father James was a tailor, his mother Alma Taylor a housewife.

After he completed grade eleven in St John's, he worked with Job Brothers before he joined the Rangers in 1935. He joined the force largely to make a better life for himself.

In April 1938, he married Janet Hardiman and they had two children; Roger and Marilyn. After leaving the Rangers in 1943 he worked in various management positions with companies such as the Royal Stores and the Canadian National Institute for the Blind.

#28

Regimental Number 28 - Ian Glendinning

Ian Glendinning is certainly one of Mount Pearl's most famous sons. He was born there on June 21, 1906, to Andrew and Jane "Jennie" (nee Bethune). His father operated a dairy farm on the site now occupied by the experimental farm.

Ian attended the Methodist College in St. John's and completed grade eleven there. In August 1924, he joined the staff of the Canadian Imperial Bank of Commerce and for the next nine years he worked at banks in Newfoundland and New Brunswick.

Ian's daughter, Barbara, recalls that her father joined the Rangers partly because he was in the "right place at the right time." That is, he was back in Newfoundland on business when the Rangers were recruiting. However, Barbara also wonders if her dad may have become disenchanted with nine years of working for banks.

"All his life Dad had a deep love of the outdoors and of adventure. He likely saw that employment with the Rangers would allow him a more interesting career," Barbara says.

Ian spent fifteen years in the Rangers and served at detachments in Forteau, Battle Harbour in Labrador, Burin and St. John's.

Two remarkable events happened while he was in the Ranger Force. First, he married Dorothy Miller on October 18, 1937. Ian had to get permission to leave Battle Harbour for the wedding. Dorothy later traveled to Battle Harbour aboard the Northern Ranger.

A second great event that happened to Ian occurred when he was promoted to Captain on July 1, 1944.

Barbara recalls that her dad "had the greatest respect for the people of the North and the outports. He knew them as smart, tenacious, hardy souls, hard working and generous, living under formidable conditions and rising above their difficult circumstances."

Whenever he went on patrol he took some tinned food in his knapsack to share with local people who were suffering hardship.

Upon leaving the Rangers in 1950, he joined the RCMP where he remained until 1966. From 1959 to 1966, he was in charge of the Sydney, Nova Scotia division. When he retired, he settled in Edmonton, Alberta, where he died March 20, 1998.

Regimental Number 29 - Harry Walters

Harry Walters hailed from the small community of Petley on Random Island in Trinity Bay. His father James ran a successful general store, while his mom, Effie, tended to the household chores and the family.

#29

Harry's early education was at Petley and he went on to earn grade eleven at Bishop Feild College in St. John's. He then obtained teacher certification from Memorial University College. But he was not to be a teacher. He was among the first thirty recruits to the Newfoundland Rangers in 1935.

In September 1939, he married Mahala A. Ford at Port aux Basques. The couple raised three children; Margaret, Patricia and Barry.

Like Ian Glendinning, Harry Walters rose to the rank of Captain. After leaving the Ranger Force, Harry became the province's chief wildlife officer. He made his mark in the field creating the so-called "Walter's Wildlife Policy." which the provincial wildlife division operated under for years. That policy states that the wildlife of this province should be used to chiefly benefit its residents.

Harry had an undying love of the outdoors, no doubt furthered by his Ranger service. In fact, he died on July 24, 1967 while escorting two visiting American dignitaries to Bird Island off Witless Bay. The guests were Dr. Gabrielson and Senator Bemis.

#30

Regimental Number 30 - Howard Manstan

Howard Manstan was born in Manchester, England, to William and Malinda formerly of South Island, Placentia Bay, Newfoundland. Howard lived in England only for six months until the family relocated to St. John's where he grew up with older brother, Gordon, and a sister, Marjorie. Howard was educated at Holloway School and earned his high school diploma at Prince of Wales College.

How the family came to relocate to Newfoundland is an interesting story. It seems that Howard's dad William was a mechanic with the Rolls Royce automobile company. When Mr. Reid, owner of the Reid Newfoundland Railway, purchased two new Rolls Royce cars William Manstan was dispatched to Newfoundland to service the cars and teach Mr. Reid how to drive them. Mr. Reid later requested that William remain at the family estate on Waterford Bridge Road. Significant to note that William was one of the Blue Puttees, Number 327, in the First World War.

After completing high school, young Howard worked for two years with H.H. Marshall, a wholesale newsdealer. But the lure of the Rangers was strong and Howard left the Marshall Company in 1935 to join the newly created Force.

He had many adventures while serving in the Rangers, not the least of which was experiencing a devastating fire which destroyed his detachment at Westport on January 7, 1937, and wiped out all his supplies and materials. He left the Rangers later that year.

In May 1937 he began work as a mechanic at Terra Nova Motors in St. John's and stayed there for three years. In 1939, he married Marjorie King of Catalina and they had three children. From 1940 to 1944 he worked in the construction and contracting business, including a stint on Fort Pepperrell in St. John's. Howard later worked with the Newfoundland railroad as a welder and then, after 1949, rose to the title of Supervisor of Work Equipment with the Canadian National Railway.

In winter 1942 Howard was working near Mundy Pond in the west end of St. John's when he witnessed three lads break through the ice and fall into the water. Without thinking of his own safety, he organized a rescue party and jumped into the frigid water to pull the boys out from under the ice. No doubt his Ranger training stood him in good stead during this ordeal.

Howard passed away at the age of fifty-eight due to heart disease.

Regimental Number 31 - Burnham Gill

#31

Burnham Gill is well known to many people as the provincial archivist. However, before entering that post he was a Ranger.

Burn Gill was born in 1914 in Brigus, Conception Bay, to Ida and Dr. Frederick Gill. He was educated in Brigus and earned his grade eleven. He later went on to study journalism.

In 1936, the twenty-two year old Gill probably saw the Rangers as a great job opportunity and something of an adventure. He would later tell his family of the great camaraderie of training at Whitbourne. His younger brother Cliff was also a Ranger (# 38).

Burn served for six years as a Ranger and had many exciting and intriguing experiences. Once he almost drowned while crossing Hamilton Inlet, Labrador, by dog team. He served in St. Anthony, Port Saunders, Gambo, Gander, La Scie and North West River.

In 1941, he married Mary Saunders of Carbonear while he was stationed at La Scie. On their honeymoon, the newlyweds accompanied a mental health patient to St. John's. The couple had two daughters, Elinor and Rosalind.

After leaving the Rangers, he went back into journalism and later became the province's chief archivist. Gill did archival work for the United Church in Newfoundland and was one of the group that organized the Ranger Force Association. Without Rangers Gill, Norm Crane and John Fagan and one or two others the existence of the Ranger Force would not be known as it is today. In 2005, Gill's daughter, Elinor Ratcliffe, gave stained glass doors to The Rooms in St. John's in honour of her father.

#32

Regimental Number 32 - John Carnell

John Beverley Carnell was born October 30, 1911. His father Frank was an accountant with the Royal Stores, while his mother Violet looked after the family home at 23 Cochrane Street.

John enlisted in the Rangers in 1936 seeking adventure. He served for three years. He left in 1939 to join the 59th Heavy Artillery, attaining the rank of Sergeant.

He later married Marion Bowden but the couple did not have any children. He was employed as a salesman with Chalker and Co. in St. John's.

John passed away in Vancouver, British Columbia on February 19, 1977 aged sixty-five years. He was buried in St. John's in the Anglican cemetery on Forest Road.

#33

Regimental Number 33 - Edward Murphy

Edward Murphy was very well educated for the period in which he lived. He completed a year's training at Memorial University College.

He was born on May 21, 1915. His father Matthew was a Custom's Department Employee, while his mother Neila (nee Fitzpatrick) looked after the household and children.

Prior to joining the Rangers in August 1936, Edward was a school teacher. As a Ranger he was stationed at Bonne Bay, Deer Lake, Twillingate and Cox's Cove. In June 1939, he was a member of the Honour Guard for the Royal visit by King George VI of England and his wife Queen Elizabeth.

He left the Ranger Force in July 1941 when his contract expired. In November 1942 he married Annabelle Fairchild and they had five children: Anne; Neil; Brian; Peter; Patrick.

In the early 1940's, Edward joined the RCAF and graduated with the rank of Flight Lieutenant. While posted overseas to England, he was invalided out of the service before the war's end. He settled in British Columbia where he worked as a social worker. Later, in 1949, he returned to Newfoundland to work as Administrator of the Child Welfare Division. In 1957 he returned to Port Moody, B.C. and worked as a Social Welfare Administrator. He died October 15, 1980.

Regimental Number 34 - Walter Rockwood

Walter Rockwood was born in St. John's but grew up in Sunnyside, then called Bay Bull's Arm, Trinity Bay. His father, Arthur, ran a dry goods and confectionary shop and fished, while his mother, Blanche Pike, looked after the house and family, and ran the store.

According to his daughter Susan, Walter Rockwood dropped out of grade ten but later returned to school and completed his grade eleven. He went on to take courses in English through the International Correspondence School, and in psychology from the University of Pennsylvania.

#34

From 1933 - 1936. Rockwood was a member of the Newfoundland Constabulary and trained with the Criminal Investigation Division. From 1934 - 35, he was stationed at Nain, Labrador, and his daughter thinks he was among the first group of ten Constabulary to arrive in the "Big Land."

Walter left the Constabulary for the Rangers in 1936. Susan thinks her father loved the outdoors and the rugged Labrador lifestyle and this would have drawn him to leave the Constabulary for the Rangers.

This was the second draft of Rangers and his daughter indicates there were twenty-two in this contingent. During his Ranger service he saw action in five detachments: Port Hope Simpson, Deer Lake, Bonne Bay, Nain, Lewisporte.

While traveling to Labrador on the coastal boat, Ranger Rockwood met Seneth Miriam Rowe, a school teacher who became his wife. They were married September 24, 1940, in St. John's. They had three children: Robert, David and Susan.

Tragedy hit the Rockwood family in 1945 while living in Nain. The eldest son Robert became deaf as the result of an illness, while David died from the same illness. As a result, the family decided to move to the United States so that Robert could attend a school for the deaf. Walter Rockwood resigned from the Ranger force in 1946 after serving ten years. His conduct on his discharge certificate was listed as "exemplary."

From 1947-1948, Walter Rockwood taught at the West Virginia School for the Deaf. He later taught for two years at the Pennsylvania School for the Deaf.

From 1952-1964, he was the Director of Northern Labrador Affairs for this province. He was later approached to start a school for the deaf in the province which he did around the mid-1960s. He served as administrator for many years until his retirement in 1971.

According to his son Robert , Walter passed away in 1988 at Clarenville and is buried in Sunnyside, Trinity Bay, his boyhood home.

#35

Regimental Number 35 - Jonathan Clarence Mercer

Clarence Mercer was born in Point Leamington on December 6, 1910. His father Jonathan was an accountant, while his mother Harriett Poole kept a boarding house.

After completing grade eleven, he worked as a waiter at the Newfoundland Hotel in St. John's. He joined the Rangers in August 1936 and served for five years.

During those years he had the task, along with a fellow Ranger, of bringing out the body of Dr. Fredrick Banting following a plane crash near Gander. Banting, a Canadian physician, scientist and Nobel Laureate noted as one of the co-discoverers of insulin, was killed February 21, 1941, when the Lockheed Hudson patrol bomber in which he was traveling to England crashed shortly after takeoff from Gander.

Mercer wed Marne Tilley in 1940 and they had three daughters: Cheryl, Jennifer and Wendy.

After leaving the Rangers, he worked in the accounting departments at the U.S. bases at St. John's and Stephenville. He later became chief budget officer for Northern Radar Bases at Goose Bay.

#36

Regimental Number 36 - Eric Brown

Eric Brown was born in April 1917 in St. John's. His father Thomas was a ship owner and carpenter, his mother Rachel Mercer a housewife.

After completing grade eleven he entered the Newfoundland Constabulary where he served from June 1933 to August 1935. He resigned from the Constabulary at that time to join the Ranger Force.

As a Ranger, he saw postings to Springdale and Port Saunders and served a total of about three years. He enlisted with the Canadian Army during the Second World War and upon demobilization worked with the Department of National Revenue,

Customs and Excise, until he retired. He settled in St. John's, latterly in Montreal.

Regimental Number 37 - Nelson Forward

#37

Nelson Forward had an exemplary career as both a Ranger and a member of the RCMP. He was born in Carbonear, Conception Bay, in September 1914. His mother, Phoebe (nee Whittle), was a homemaker, while his dad Jack was a businessman. Nelson attended school in Carbonear and earned his high school diploma there.

He joined the Rangers in 1936 and stayed with the force until 1950, at which time he joined the RCMP. As a Ranger, he was stationed at Whitbourne, Kilbride, Port au Port and Port aux Basques.

Nelson married his childhood sweetheart ,Rella Simms, in 1941. The couple had five children: Pam, Robert, Joanne, Joan and Peter.

Forward's work as a Ranger was officially recognized by Magistrate Mulcahey of St. George's who wrote about the "splendidly efficient work being done by Ranger N. Forward of the Port au Port Detachment."

Not surprisingly, Nelson Forward was as excellent a Mountie as he was a Ranger. He worked all across Canada and earned the rank of Superintendent. He was an Aide- de-Camp for the Lt. Governor of British Columbia. Before he retired he was the second-in-command of the RCMP for the entire province of Newfoundland and Labrador.

After retiring from the RCMP, Nelson Forward became head of security with the Churchill Falls Power Company in Labrador. According to Pam Forward, after finishing this work, her parents retired to their hometown of Carbonear and built a house overlooking the harbour.

Nelson Forward passed away on July 6, 1994. His wife, Rella, died on March 4, 2003.

#38

Regimental Number 38 - Clifford Gill

Clifford Gill became a Newfoundland Ranger in 1936 and served for ten years. He was born in Brigus, the son of Dr. Fredrick Gill. He received his early education in Brigus and completed high school at St. Bonaventure's College in St. John's. After high school, he went to sea as a merchant seaman. When he was rejected by the Army because of childhood polio he joined the Rangers. He was posted to Recontre West, Badger and Point Leamington. Around 1940, he wed Grace Bragg and they had two daughters; Rosemary and Elizabeth.

After leaving the Rangers, he ran a nightclub in Botwood in central Newfoundland. Later he became the Registrar of the College of the North Atlantic in Grand Falls. He was the brother of Burnham Gill, Ranger # 31.

#39

Regimental Number 39 - Gordon Butler

Gordon Butler was part of the second contingent of Rangers. This St. John's man was born on August 27, 1910, to Henry and Jane (nee Stead). He was educated at Bishop Feild College in St. John's where he earned grade eleven.

Prior to joining the Rangers he worked with Bowring Brothers in St. John's. But in 1936, with economic opportunities scarce and his mother and five siblings hurting from the death of his father, Gordon, as the eldest in the family, joined the Rangers with his good friend John Carnell. He served 5-1/2 years as a Ranger and was posted to Fortune, Deer Lake and Lamaline.

He left the Rangers to enter the Royal Air Force (RAF) in 1941. During the war he met a lovely English lass who was to play a big part in his life. He was discharged after WWII and on June 27, 1946, he married J. Denise Buller of England. Together, the couple had three children: Wendy Philips, Gillian Butler and Mark Butler. From 1946 to 1967, Gordon worked in commerce to support his family.

Denise Butler writes that "even though she did not know her husband while he was in the Ranger Force he spoke of his years as a Ranger often and had many mementoes of his service. He made many friends who remained his friends until his death in 1967."

Regimental Number 40 - Michael Delahunty

Michael Joseph Delahunty was born in Calvert on the Irish Southern Shore of the Avalon Peninsula. He came into the world on April 25, 1912.

He was a member of the second contingent of Rangers and joined in 1936. But it is unclear exactly when he left the Rangers.

According to his nephew, Brian, after he left the Rangers, Michael was employed at the American base in St. John's. While working at Fort Pepperrell, base records indicate that Michael was an exemplary employee and held several posts

#40

including to the Chief of the Pay Branch where he was responsible for maintaining military and civilian pay records.

He later operated a small convenience store on Water Street West. Along the road of life he married Ethel Goff.

Michael and Ethel later worked with Terra Nova National Park as administrators. After leaving the park they operated a senior citizens home in Harbour Grace known as the Grand Haven. He died in May, 1978. His brother was Ranger # 9, Joseph Delahunty.

Regimental Number 41 - Gladstone Guzzwell

Gladstone "Glad" Guzzwell figured prominently in Horwood's History of the Ranger Force. Glad was born on June 14, 1917, to Ernest and Annie (nee Edgecombe). Ernest was a cabbie with a horse and buggy, while Annie looked after the home and family. The Guzzwells later owned and ran a farm on Logy Bay Road, St. John's.

Glad was educated at the old Centenary Hall School in St. John's and earned grade eleven. Before joining the Rangers in 1936, he worked on the family farm. The Rangers provided the promise of adventure and a steady job, a bright light in the dim 1930s.

Guzzwell served a five year hitch with the Rangers and was posted to Burin, Badger, Port aux Basques, Forteau, Marystown, North West River, Nain and Hebron.

While still a Ranger, he married Irene Pye of Cape Charles, Labrador. They were joined in matrimony on June 18, 1940, in Forteau, Labrador. The couple had three sons: Melvin, Keith and Geoffrey.

One very exciting experience Glad had as a Ranger was being at the centre of the Marystown "riot" of 1938. As recounted by Harold Horwood, Rangers Guzzwell and Rex Dingwall were on duty when a mob of more than one hundred people surrounded the detachment and threatened to put the Rangers on the boat back to St. John's. But Guzzwell and Dingwall stood the unruly mob down. Guzzwell told Horwood: "I went out with a baton in one pocket and a revolver in the other and I was determined that nobody was going to lay a hand on me that morning."

After leaving the Rangers in 1941, Guzzwell worked on the construction of Fort Pepperrell in St. John's and during the war years operated a successful taxi cab like his father.

In 1950 he was awarded a contract to provide trucking service to Canada Post in St. John's. After about 12 yeas he was made Postal Fleet Supervisor, a position he retired from in 1982. The Guzzwells remained in St. John's during Glad's retirement. His brother Harold was Ranger # 23.

Regimental Number 42 - Josiah Clarke

#42

Josiah Clarke hailed from the scenic Conception Bay town of Bishop's Cove. He was born on November 8, 1914, to Issac and Winnifred Clarke. Issac was a hardy fisherman, while Winnie looked after the home and family.

The young Josiah attended school in Bishop's Cove where he obtained his grade eleven. He joined the Rangers in 1936 and served for a few years, but it is thought that, for whatever reason, he did not complete the five year Ranger contract.

Josiah married Blanche Smith on July 1, 1942, and they had three children: Vera, George and Joan. After leaving the Rangers, Josiah worked as a carpentry contractor in the Conception Bay South area. He passed away on May 14, 1992.

Regimental Number 43 - Nelson Goulding

#43

Nelson Goulding was the son of Anglo-Newfoundland Development Company mill worker Garfield and his wife Isabella (nee Saunders). He was born in 1913 in Bishop's Falls and educated at Grand Falls Academy where he earned his high school diploma. He had one brother, Charlie, and four sisters Greta, Lucy, Edwina and Anne.

He joined the Rangers in 1936 and was stationed at several detachments including Glenwood, Burgeo, Flowers Cove, St. Anthony and Stephenville Crossing. After five years of service he re-enlisted with the Rangers. His brother Charlie was also a Ranger (#108).

In 1941, he married Kathleen Christian but the couple did not have any children. He left the Ranger Force in October 1943.

After leaving the Rangers, Nelson joined the Halifax Police Department in Nova Scotia. He served as a motorcycle patrolman. When he retired from the Halifax Police Force in 1973 he had risen to the rank of Detective Sgt. and was awarded a 29-year service award.

From 1973 to 1983 he was a fraud inspector with Royal Bank of Canada in Halifax. He passed away on April 19, 1983 in Halifax. He is buried in Our Lady of Mount Carmel Cemetery, in Prospect, Nova Scotia.

Regimental Number 44 - Ewart Peckford

Ewart Peckford is perhaps most well known for being the father of former Newfoundland Premier Brian Peckford. But Ewart was also a Ranger.

He was born in St. John's on October 9, 1912, to Joseph, a fisherman, and Clara (Brett). Ewart attended Bishop Feild College and also Butler Brothers, a private commercial school. He earned grade eleven and a commercial course; high education for those times.

#44

Prior to joining the Rangers, Ewart worked as clerk and book-keeper with Marine Agencies. But the adventure and opportunity promised by the Rangers proved strong and so he joined up in 1936. On July 5, 1939, he married Allison Young and they had six children: Bruce, Brian, Sydney, Lawrence, Brenda and Ian.

Ewart Peckford must have shown quite a potential. The young Ranger was selected to complete an eight month RCMP training program which included finger-printing and photography, among other police work. Then he was promoted to the rank of Staff Sgt. and thereafter had a hand in training recruits to the Ranger Force at headquarters in Whitbourne and Kilbride.

Ewart Peckford stayed with the Rangers until 1949. After leaving the Rangers he worked as a businessman, a social worker and nursing home superintendent.

He passed away on January 4, 1992.

#45

Regimental Number 45 - Robin Sparkes

Robin Sparkes was a Ranger for eight years, serving until 1943. He was born in Whitbourne (where the first Rangers trained) in 1911. Robin's father, George, was a customs officer/postmaster and ran a general store, while his mother Emiline Rodway was a midwife.

Robin completed his high school education in Whitbourne and after joining the Rangers was stationed at various detachments including Fortune, Twillingate, Rose Blanche and Lewisporte.

Robin recalls the dangerous work of having to travel offshore over sea-ice to inspect steam ships for customs duties. He recalls that on one occasion while traveling by dog team the team, sled and he himself all broke through thin ice and hit the water, but made it out safely in large part thanks to the dogs who were good swimmers.

In October 1941, he married Joyce Roberts from Twillingate and the couple had three children: Laurie (Larry), Sandra (Herold) and Cheryl Lynn (Clark). Today, these three offspring have flowered into a large family circle of 4 grand-children and eight great-grandchildren. Robin and Joyce celebrated their 63rd wedding anniversary in October 2004. Robin turned 94 in January 2005 as this book was being written.

After leaving the Rangers, Robin and Joyce settled in his home town of Whitbourne until they moved to the United States in 1946. The main reason they moved was to join other family members in the New York State area. Robin finally settled in Rochester, N.Y. in 1958. He was employed as a machinist at Gleason Works until his retirement in 1976.

#46

Regimental Number 46 - Matt Davis

Matt Davis was born in Argentia on June 30, 1914. His father James was a fish merchant, while his mother, Margaret (Murphy), owned and operated a hotel and grocery store and was also a postmistress.

After finishing high school, he worked with the family business. He joined the Rangers on July 3, 1936. He was stationed at Burin and Hebron. He served for five years and left the Rangers in 1941. Following his retirement from the Ranger Force he owned and operated a butcher shop in Dunville.

In 1945, he wed Hilda Bennett and they had five children: Patricia, William (deceased); Peggy (deceased); Elaine and Maureen.

In 1947, he moved to Holyrood and operated "The Bennet's Inn." Following a fire the name was changed to "Davis Club."

Regimental Number 47 - Harry Tapper

#47

Henry "Harry" Tapper was born in June 1914 in Lomond on the beautiful west coast of Newfoundland. His father John was a clerk while his mother Sarah was a homemaker.

Harry completed grade eleven and also studied forestry, making him highly educated for the time. He joined the Rangers in 1936 for the adventure and steady employment.

On August 30, 1938, Harry married Florence Leonard aboard the SS Northern Ranger. At the time he was stationed at Forteau and enroute there with his intended bride when Rev. (later Canon) Richards visited the ship off Flowers Cove and they decided to marry there and then. The couple had a daughter, Anne, and it was unable to be confirmed whether or not they also had a son.

After leaving the Rangers, Harry was employed with the Woods Management Division of Bowaters Paper Company in Corner Brook. He was later transferred to New Zealand. He and his wife settled in Auckland, New Zealand, where Harry died in October 1995.

Regimental Number 48 - Herbert Tucker

#48

All the Rangers had unique backgrounds, none more so than Herbert Tucker who hailed from Glace Bay, Nova Scotia. Herbert was born on October 19, 1916. His dad Walter was a coal miner with the Dominion Collieries while his mother Minnie (nee Janes) was a homemaker.

Herbert was raised by relatives in Port de Grave, Newfoundland following the untimely death of both his parents.

He joined the Rangers in August 1936 and was stationed in Fortune, Twillingate, Nain, Hopedale and at headquarters.

One sad experience Herbert had was in Labrador when a team of Huskies killed a young Inuit boy. The dogs had to be destroyed by the youthful Ranger. Herbert served a total of five years and two months as a Ranger and left the force on October 13, 1941.

Almost precisely a year after leaving the Rangers, Herbert married Susanna Douglas. The couple had five children: Herbert; Douglas; Barbara; Katherine and Colleen.

After retiring from the Rangers, Herbert joined the Royal Air Force (RAF) where he graduated as flight officer/navigator. He remained with the RAF until 1945 and was awarded 5 service medals. Herbert remained part of the RAF reserve until 1952.

After the war ended, he was employed as an office manager by the Department of National Defence at Point Edward Naval Base in Cape Breton, Nova Scotia. The couple settled in nearby Westmount, Cape Breton. Herbert passed away on January 9, 1976.

#49

Regimental Number 49 - Michael Greene

Michael Greene was another Ranger who came from the ranks of the Newfoundland Constabulary. Sadly, he was also one of three Rangers to die while on duty.

He was born in 1914 in Placentia Bay. His father Michael was a coastal purser on the Newfoundland Railway ships, while his mother Mary (nee Tobin) was a homemaker. Michael, who never married, remained with the Ranger Force for 2-1/2 years until he was killed as a result of a tragic accident.

On March 5, 1939, while on patrol near Lorries (now Point May) the horse and sled he was traveling on broke through the ice on a pond. Ranger Greene managed to get out of the frigid water but perished a short distance away.

Like Danny Corcoran (No. 14) and Michael Collins (No. 166), Michael Greene made the ultimate sacrifice while carrying out his Ranger duties.

Regimental Number 50 - Dawson Bishop

Dawson Bishop was born in St. John's in 1912, the son of Walter and Alice (nee Cooper) Bishop. After completion of high school at Prince of Wales College he joined the Newfoundland Constabulary and remained a policeman for two years.

#50

He joined the Rangers in August 1936 and saw postings to Flower's Cove, Marystown, Glenwood and Twillingate. He served as a Ranger for seven years and attained the rank of Sergeant. He left the force in 1943. He later wed Ruth Clarke and they had four sons: William, Wilson, George and James.

Regimental Number 51 - Edward Thorburn

Edward "Ted" Thorburn was born in St. John's on June 26, 1916. His parents were Tom and Josephine (nee Thorburn). Ed completed grade eleven at St. Bonaventure's College and immediately joined the Rangers. He was posted to Marystown, Badger and Lamaline.

#51

Ted was attracted to the rugged outdoor life and the chance for a career in law enforcement. He remained a Ranger for about eight years.

In June, he married Eileen Shanahan of Riverhead and they had a large family of nine children: Tom; Judy; Bonaventure; Edward; Maureen; Eileen; Kathy; Paula; and Frank.

After leaving the Rangers, Ted supported his family by working with the Motor Vehicle Branch of the Provincial Government.

Ted passed away on October 31, 1992, while Eileen died on August 22, 1994. Coincidentally, Edward Jr. is in law enforcement too; he is a fishery officer in British Columbia where his parents had settled.

Regimental Number 52 - Charles Jerrett

#52

Charles "Charlie" Jerrett was born at Clarke's Beach on November 29, 1915, to Emma and Fred. His father was a fishermen who went to the Labrador for many years and fished out of Indian Harbour. Charlie earned his school diploma at school in Clarke's Beach. After completing grade eleven he joined the ranks of the Newfoundland Constabulary.

But the promise of better pay and benefits, plus an adventure in outport detachments drew the fisherman's son into the Ranger Force. "It was something new I guess," he says. Charlie was unsure of the precise year he joined the Force, but it was in the second draft. He remembers the physical Ranger training of running for miles every morning. He was stationed at Burgeo and St. Lawrence.

In October 1942, he married Elsie Coveyduck, and they had two daughters, Linda and June. After leaving the Ranger Force, Charlie went to work on the American base at Argentia. He retired to New Haven, Connecticut, where he passed away July 16, 2005.

Charlie Jerrett had one very close call while serving in Burgeo that he can't forget. He was on patrol at Grand Bruit in the winter and had to make it back to Burgeo the next day to administer the "dole" or relief. He engaged a guide who knew the country to accompany him on the long walk to Burgeo. After walking open country of bogs and marshes for several hours a driving snowstorm came upon them. The guide was unsure of the way to go in the drifting snow, but Ranger Jerrett knew they had to find some trees if they were to survive the blizzard.

As they struggled against the howling wind they finally came to a grove of trees. As they entered the woods to seek a place to build a shelter they realized that the trees were completely covered in snow making it impossible to start a fire. As they searched for the most sheltered spot, they couldn't believe their eyes. They saw a light. As they began to walk towards it they realized that it was the light peeking through the board sides of a trapper's shack.

When they banged on the door the trapper opened it and welcomed them in. Charlie Jerrett says, "The Good Lord had to be with us throughout this day to guide us to this glimmer of light in a shack at night." The next day the storm was over and Ranger Jerrett and his guide proceeded to Burgeo. No doubt things could have gone quite differently for Jerrett and his guide. Had they not happened upon the trapper's shack, they may have perished.

Regimental Number 53 - Jasper Suley

It is no wonder Jasper Suley joined the Rangers. You see he was born in Whitbourne, the first headquarters of the Rangers on November 5, 1916. His father Robert worked for the Newfoundland Railway, while his mom Hannah (nee Crane) looked after the house and family.

Jasper earned his grade eleven in Whitbourne and joined the Ranger Force on June 7, 1937. He was posted to various detachments including Battle Harbour, St. Anthony and Port Hope Simpson. He served with the Rangers for 3-1/2 years and left the Force on December 3, 1940.

#53

After leaving the Rangers, he joined the Royal Air Force (RAF) and stayed until the end of WWII as a wireless operator. After demobilization, he was employed with Gander Air Radio Signals (now Nav Canada).

He married Marion (Newell) in February 1947 and they had five children: Richard, Wayne, Donna, Neil and Cathy. The couple lived in Gander, where Jasper worked. He died November 15, 1987.

Regimental Number 54 - Colin George

Colin George was another fisherman's son-turned-Ranger. He was born in New Harbour, Trinity Bay, to Edmund and Emily (Brinston). He earned grade eleven in New Harbour but the promise of adventure in the Rangers lured him to join the Force in 1937. He served in outport detachments like Cartwright and Jackson's Arm.

Colin served in the Rangers for about two years and left the force to join the RAF. He married Leana Outerbridge of Bermuda and they had two children - Kevin and Verna.

#54

After the end of the war the Georges settled in sunny Bermuda where Colin operated a garment/clothing store.

#55

Regimental Number 55 - Rex Dingwall

Bob Dingwall says that his father talked a lot about the time he spent in the Newfoundland Rangers. "It was an important event in his life," Bob says.

Rex Dingwall served at least ten years in the Rangers and during that time made the first known wildlife patrol by fixed wing aircraft in Newfoundland. It seems that Dingwall was serving on the southwest coast and received reports of caribou being poached on the Lewis Hills. He engaged a visiting pilot with a two-seater open cockpit plane to fly him over the hills to survey the situation. Rex Dingwall also handled the first murder case investigated by the Rangers while he was stationed at Port au Port.

Dingwall was born in 1914 in Channel, Newfoundland. He was one of ten children in the family of carpenter John Dingwall and his wife Violet.

After leaving school Rex worked for two years with the local doctor as an "office boy." One job he used to do was sterilizing bottles. He also delivered prescriptions. After this work he was employed with the merchant firm of E. Pike Ltd. The Pikes thought so highly of Dingwall they offered to double his salary if he stayed with them instead of joining the Rangers.

But the lure of the Rangers proved strong and Rex Dingwall joined up in 1937.

He was posted to various detachments including Whitbourne, Burin, Marystown, Port au Port, St. Anthony, and Bonne Bay. Rex told his son Bob he'd always wanted to be a policeman.

Rex served two five year terms as a Ranger and retired as a Sergeant. The Ranger training stuck with Rex and he often talked about it. In particular he spoke highly of the medical training that Dr. Newhook and Dr. Cluny MacPherson offered to the young Rangers.

Rex married his wife Netta on January 8, 1940. They had two children Bob and Marilyn.

When he requested a discharge from the Rangers in 1947 a report described him as a "conscientious, reliable, trustworthy member." This report also stated that if he wished to re-engage for a further period his application would have been approved.

After leaving the Rangers, Rex went into the wholesale business and worked for many years as a manufacturer's agent.

Regimental Number 56 - William Smith

William J. "Bill" Smith joined the Rangers on July 5, 1937. He was not yet twenty-seven years-old. He is the father of co-author Robert Smith.

Bill was born in Brigus, Conception Bay, on September 21, 1910. He was the second of three children born to Michael Smith and Cecilia Smith (nee Woodford). Michael was trained as a gas engineer, worked as a superintendent in the Cape Breton Mines and later ran a business in Georgetown-Marysvale, Conception Bay. Cecilia was an accomplished commercial artist.

#56

Bill got his early schooling in Sydney, Nova Scotia, and Brigus, and then completed grade twelve at St. Bonaventure's College in St. John's. He worked in the family business for ten years before entering the Rangers.

Bill remained a Ranger for 11 years, 2 months and 2 days. By the time he left the Rangers he was the Sgt.-in-charge for western Newfoundland. While a Ranger, he served in Bonne Bay, Deer Lake, Stephenville Crossing and St. Georges.

In 1945, Bill, along with Sgt Nelson Forward, was sent to the RCMP training depot in Regina, Saskatchewan, for advanced police training.

During his service in St. George's, Bill met and courted Mary Kelloway who was a Registered Nurse in charge of the Stephenville Cottage Hospital. They married on June 18, 1942, and had four children: Robert - a provincial court judge; Rosemary - a teacher; Cecilia - a registered nurse; Olivia - a social worker.

In September 1948, Bill resigned from his much beloved force to enter university and study towards admission to law school. On his discharge certificate, Major Martin, Chief Ranger, wrote "During his period of service to the Newfoundland Ranger Force, William Smith proved to be a most conscientious, reliable and trustworthy officer."

Bill entered Dalhousie Law School and graduated in 1953 with a law degree. He won two major scholarships during his tenure at "Dal" including the "Olive Moore McEvoy Scholarship."

In his graduating year, Bill teamed with future Nova Scotia Court of Appeals Justice, David Chipman, to win the "Smith Shield." This award recognized the best legal argument in a Court of Appeal setting by graduating students.

After graduation, Bill articled with R.A. Parsons in St. John's. Following admission to the Law Society of Newfoundland, he moved to Corner Brook where he assumed the practice of the Hon. L. Whelan.

One of his first cases in Corner Brook involved Bill representing well-known businessman and Deputy Mayor, Al Kawaja, in a libel suit against the Bowaters-owned Western Star newspaper. The case was successful and turned up as a precedent to be studied at law school. In time, Bill developed a busy litigation and criminal practice.

In 1954, Bill accepted a partnership in law with future Justice of the Supreme Court, Mr. Kevin Barry. They practiced under the name Barry and Smith for ten years.

In addition to a professional presence in Corner Brook, Bill Smith was an ardent volunteer. He was active in the Knights of Columbus, serving as both Grand Knight and Faithful Navigator. He also worked with the SPCA, St. John Ambulance, Rotary Club, Regina High School PTA, Western Memorial Hospital, Victorian Order of Nurses and was co-chair of the 1964 Catholic Regional Social Life conference.

Bill was also actively involved in politics in the hopes of transforming for the better his beloved Newfoundland. The Hon. W.J. Browne, M.P., Solicitor General for Canada, visited Bill and urged him to seek election in the Humber-St. George's District for the House of Commons.
Bill secured the nomination but lost the election to future Deputy Speaker of the House of Commons, Herman Batten.

Undeterred, Bill ran in provincial politics in 1962 and he won the outport seat of St. Barbe South defeating the Hon. Max Lane in the process. This victory made Smith the first Progressive Conservative MHA elected in the outports of Newfoundland. Previously, the PC's had only held seats on the Avalon Peninsula.

As a politician, Bill Smith carried his Ranger's courtesy, fortitude and social conscience with him. He fought for better conditions in the logging camps, he helped fishermen cut through red tape and he advocated the necessity of expanding the tourism sector as an economic development tool. He called for the creation of a National Park at the entrance to Bonne Bay, now the site of Gros Morne National Park.

In August 1965, Bill met his earthly end when he died of an apparent heart attack minutes before a Magistrate's Court appearance. But right to the end, Bill Smith was serving others. The day before he died he witnessed a young child set a parked car in motion. Bill ran and jumped into the vehicle bringing it to a stop before it shot out into traffic.

At his death, the editor of the Western Star, William Callahan, wrote a column called "A Good Man Passes."

If there was ever a man for the underdog, it was he. There is little doubt his intensity of feeling contributed to his passing at an early age."

After Bill's death, his widow Mary returned to nursing and became a nursing supervisor at Western Hospital in Corner Brook. She passed away in 1994.

Regimental Number 57 - Ernest Clarke

#57

Ernest Clarke was not only a Ranger but the editor/owner of a newspaper in Twillingate. He was born in Twillingate on June 19, 1917. His father Lewis was a sail-maker and his mother Lydia looked after the family and home.

Before he entered the Rangers, Ernest proved himself to be a brave young man. At age eighteen he rescued a young girl, Gwen Cook, from the icy waters of Twillingate Harbour. He was awarded the Boy Scout's medal in recognition of his gallantry.

Ernest earned grade eleven at St. Peter's School in Twillingate. He then worked in a general store but the storekeeper's life proved too dull for the young man. So, he joined the Rangers in 1937.

Over the course of the next ten years, Ernest would be stationed in Bay L'Argent, Grand Bank, Port Hope Simpson, Port Saunders, Hopedale, Cartwright, Nain and Springdale.

Clarke attained the rank of Corporal. However, on June 29, 1945, he was appointed Government Agent in Northern Labrador with temporary rank of Inspector. After this post was abolished in 1946, he returned to the island portion of the province and was promoted to Sergeant.

After five years of service he wed Ada Minty. They had one son Peter. Ernest also penned a tongue-in-cheek poem which poked some fun at the men who went through Ranger training with him. The last of ten verses is as follows:

> 'Tis over now - we had our fun
> There never was a better bunch of men,
> As one who knew, I'd like to say,
> We shall not see their like again - (Thank God)

Ern Clarke had a strong affection for Labrador and its people. While stationed there in the 1940's he wrote an article to a Canadian newspaper entitled "be it ever so Humble," the first paragraph of which reflects his sentiments. It too reads as follows:

Be it ever so humble there's no place like home. And to Uncle Sam Blake and his wife Lottie, their dilapidated cabin of rough hewn logs, burrowed into the side of a hill in a sheltered bay in Labrador, was as precious a possession as the finest mansion to its millionaire owner.

After leaving the Rangers, Ernest became editor of the Twillingate Sun newspaper, a post he held for several years. Eventually he became the owner of the paper, a position he held until his untimely death at age fifty.

Regimental Number 58 - Roy Manuel

Roy Manuel hailed from Twillingate's shores. He was born September 9, 1909, to Alfred and Frances (nee Freeman). Alfred was a carpenter and also a Purser with the Newfoundland Railway.

He earned grade eleven at St. Peter's Anglican School in Twillingate. After leaving school he worked as a carpenter with his dad and later as an undertaker in Toronto.

Roy joined the Rangers in 1937 and served for ten years. He was stationed in Cartwright, Belleoram and Springdale. When he left the Rangers in 1947 he held the rank of Corporal.

In 1940 he married Edith Simms. She later received the Order of Canada. The couple made their mark on their adopted home of Springdale where they owned and operated a building supplies store. They were involved with the Sea Cadet Corps, the volunteer Fire Hall, the Lion's Club, the Anglican Church and the town council, on which Roy served a full term. In 1991, the town's community hall was named "The Manuel Community Hall" in recognition of Edith and Roy's record of community service.

By a strange twist of fate, the Manuels also established a funeral parlor in the town of Springdale and Roy was the first to lie in wake there on Oct. 19, 1978.

#59

Regimental Number 59 - Dean Bragg

Percival Dean Bragg was born at Channel on October 2, 1915. His mother, Blanche (White), was a homemaker, while his father, Edwin, was a Newfoundland Railway employee and later a game warden.

Dean earned his grade eleven from school in Port aux Basques and joined the Rangers in 1937. He was posted to St. George's, Hopedale and Nain. While stationed in Hopedale, he investigated the untimely deaths of three men who died from starvation after their aircraft crashed in the interior of Labrador. This was written about in the St. John's "Daily News" on October 24, 1940.

He stayed with the Rangers for five years and left the force in 1942 when he enlisted in the Royal Canadian Naval Volunteer Reserve. He attained the rank of Lieutenant.

In 1944, he married Emily Marguerite (Green) and they had two children, Michele and Michael.

After the end of WWII., he was employed with the British Columbia Department of Transportation in air surveying. During the Korean War, he re-enlisted with the RCNVR with the rank of Lieut. Commander and served three years in Cornwallis and Shearwater, Nova Scotia. After the end of the war he returned to his work in British Columbia.

Regimental Number 60 - David Howley

David Howley was born in St. John's on December 23, 1916, to James and Mary (Walsh) Howley. David's father carried the honour of being a Member of the British Empire (MBE).

David was educated at St. Bon's and Memorial University College and joined the Rangers in July 1937. He was stationed at headquarters in Whitbourne and St. George's. He remained a Ranger for about 3-1/2 years, at which time he entered the armed forces.

He enlisted in the RCAF and earned the rank of Pilot Officer. After the end of hostilities he entered

#60

McGill University and earned a commerce degree. In 1950, he wed nurse Constance (Consie) McCartney and they had five children: Katherine, David, Virginia, Constance and Richard. He was Newfoundland's Auditor General from 1968 to 1980.

Regimental Number 61 - Eric Stickland

Of all the Newfoundland Rangers who had diverse post-Ranger careers Eric Stickland surely had one of the most interesting. Eric was a Pilot Officer in the Royal Canadian Air Force during the Second World War and later served as a station manager with Air France. No doubt his flying career had lots of ups and downs!

Eric was born in Grand Bank on August 10, 1912. His father Albert was a Salvation Army Major, while his mother Druscilla (nee Beston) was a Salvation Army Captain. Eric was a student

#61

at Prince of Wales College where he earned grade eleven. He also completed some advanced training at Memorial University College before becoming a school teacher. But the teacher's life was not for Eric Stickland. In 1937, he joined the Newfoundland Rangers.

He served four years as a Ranger and was posted to Port aux Basques, Burgeo and Belleoram.

In August 1941, the pipes of war called him off the roster of the Rangers and drew him into the ranks of the RCAF. After the war ended he married Marjorie Gridley and they had two children Eric and Sara. He put his flight training to good work after the war when he joined Air France. After he retired he settled in the States, in sunny Arizona. He died August 2, 1996.

Regimental Number 62 - Frederick Thompson

#62

Frederick "Fred" Thompson was born in St. John's on December 14, 1917. His father, Frederick, worked with the Standard Manufacturing Company and his mother, Louise (Williams), was a homemaker.

Fred was educated at St. Bon's College and earned grade eleven with honors. He joined the Rangers in August 1937 and was posted to detachments in Codroy, Badger and Port aux Basques. In 1940, he wed Margaret Tompkins and they had three children: Terrence, Carl and Mark.

In 1942, he left the Rangers with an honourable discharge. At the time the Chief Ranger wrote that, "His work at all times was of a very excellent standard, and had he elected to remain with the Force would have attained N.C.O.'s rank. His character was exemplary."

Fred later became a radio operator with the RCAF and Transport Canada. In 1971, he retired from Transport Canada as Inspector-in-Charge, Radio Regulations, Newfoundland and Labrador.

Regimental Number 63 - Leslie Ledrew

#63

Leslie Ledrew was the son of schooner skipper George Ledrew of Change Islands and Augusta (nee Hoff), a homemaker. Leslie was born on September 15, 1913, and educated at Laurenceton School and Prince of Wales College in St. John's. After completing his schooling he was employed as a school teacher, but the adventure promised by the Ranger Force proved too much and he enlisted in 1937.

In 1941, he married Mildred Tetford and they had a large family: George, David; Larry; Bevin; Lorne; William; and Roy, who died in infancy.

Leslie remained a Ranger for 13 years, leaving only when the Force was absorbed into the RCMP in 1950. During his time as a Ranger he was stationed in Englee, Glenwood, Norris Arm, and St. Lawrence.

Leslie had his own unique challenges to deal with. He suffered from a hearing impairment and in order to travel to Canada for surgery, he had to sell a house he had built while in the Ranger Force.

After leaving the Rangers, he owned and operated a poultry farm for many years. He also worked as outdoors foreman with Alyward's Ltd. of St. Lawrence. He retired to St. John's.

Regimental Number 64 - Edward Power

#64

Edward Power was a St. John's man through and through. He was born in the city on May 15, 1914, and lived at 54 Mullock Street. He was named after his father who was an engineer. His mother Rosalie was the owner-operator of Power's Confectionary on Hayward Avenue.

Edward was educated at St. Patrick's Hall School and completed a commercial course offered by well-known Brother T.I. Murphy. He graduated from this course around 1932.

Prior to serving as a Ranger, Edward worked at Whitbourne as a civilian in the Ranger office. He was asked to join the Rangers.

The time Edward spent in Whitbourne was important because he not only joined the Newfoundland Rangers, but he also met his wife, Marie Foley from Whitbourne. The couple had two sons; Brian and David.

David is a Provincial Court Judge, while contributor Robert Smith claims Ed Power as his Godfather.

After the Rangers were absorbed into the RCMP, Edward joined the Mounties and attained the rank of Staff Sgt. Major. He was the first Newfoundland Ranger to earn this rank in the RCMP.

After retiring from the RCMP, Edward was a tireless volunteer. He worked with young offenders teaching them how to refinish furniture, his hobby. He was also a blood donor for many years and was on the call list for the Red Cross.

Regimental Number 65 - Eric Noseworthy

#65

Eric Noseworthy was the subject of a touching article in The Telegram by Jean Edwards Stacey. The information here comes from that story.

Eric was born in 1914 in Spaniard's Bay where he received his early education. His parents were Lorenzo and Mary. He completed his education at Bishop Feild College in St. John's and then went to work with a business on Water Street.

Noseworthy joined the Rangers in 1937 and stayed with the Force until 1950, at which time he joined the RCMP. As a Ranger, he saw service in several communities including Lewisporte, Harbour Breton and Battle Harbour, Labrador.

As a Mountie, he served in Corner Brook and earned the rank of Corporal before retiring in 1965. After leaving the RCMP he was a Justice of the Peace and Deputy Registrar of Motor Vehicles in Corner Brook.

Noseworthy's first wife was Margaret Paul of Lawn, Placentia Bay. She died of cancer in 1983. In 1985, he married Lenora Fox, a widow whose husband, Roland, had died in 1977. Noseworthy and his second wife settled in Gander.

Noseworthy's stepson, Jack Fox, recalls that Eric was a real sportsman who loved to hunt and fish for trout and salmon. He also enjoyed a good game of cribbage. Eric passed away on June 11, 2004.

Eric's son, Fred, is a Colonel in the Canadian Forces and has distinguished himself as a professional engineer throughout the world. Fred has been presented to the Queen. Eric's brother, also Fred, was Ranger # 19.

Regimental Number 66 - Charles Holland

Charles Holland was one of ten children born to Alma (Hoberg) and Michael Holland. Charles was born in 1916 and completed high school in St. John's. He also finished a two year business program at the school.

Prior to joining the Rangers, Charles made a trip to the ice, seal hunting, so he knew firsthand about surviving outdoors in tough conditions. No doubt this experience came in handy when he was a Ranger. But the main reason he joined the Rangers in 1937 was to secure a steady income for himself.

He remained a Ranger for about four years, but like several of his contemporaries, he left the Force to join the RAF. However, he also told his children how difficult it was administering the dole during the great depression as a Ranger.

After the war's end, Sgt. Holland retired to St. John's where he met and married Isabel (Brigham) in 1948. Over the course of the rest of his working career, Charles put his business training to good use and worked as an accountant with firms in Ontario and New Brunswick. His last position was as director of finance for the government of P.E.I.'s hospital and health services commission. Charles passed away on November 4, 1992.

Regimental Number 67 - Gilbert Jenkins

Gilbert "Bert" Jenkins was born in Woody Point on April 1, 1917. His father Malcolm was a customs collector, while his mother Susannah was a homemaker.

Bert earned his grade eleven in Woody Point and joined the Rangers in 1937. As a Ranger, he was posted to various detachments including Deer Lake, Lamaline and Burin. His brother Tom was Ranger # 199.

On December 29, 1941, Bert married Emma Mary Noseworthy. They had two children Jacqueline and Terrence.

#67

Following Confederation, Bert joined the RCMP and served with that Force until his retirement in 1968 with the rank of Staff Sergeant. He then worked with the provincial government in the departments of tourism and labour. When he retired a second time, he settled in St. John's where he passed away on January 22, 2001.

#68

Regimental Number 68 - Eric Toms

Eric Toms was born October 21, 1916, at La Scie to Jonathon Toms, fisherman, and Lydia (Sheppard) Toms, housewife. He received his schooling in La Scie and completed grade eleven there. Armed with his high school diploma he began teaching school. He taught for a number of years before joining the Rangers.

Eric joined the Rangers in 1938 and was stationed in Deer Lake and Flowers Cove among other places. He served his five year hitch and left the Force in 1943.

A year late, in 1944, he married Margaret Hill, and they had two sons, David and Eric. After marrying, Eric moved his family to the small Quebec mining town of West Malartic, where he worked for about five years as a surveyor and geological technician. About 1950 he went into business with his older brother Ross and together they began prospecting all over Northern and Central Canada in search of precious minerals such as iron ore, uranium, silver, copper and other metals. Eric found many significant deposits over the years but at no point did he strike it rich.

He gradually retired from prospecting in the early 1980s. He was tragically killed in a car accident while on his way to his beloved cabin in Newfoundland.

His sons recall that Eric was a quiet man who did not say much about his past life so their knowledge of his time in the Rangers is limited.

#69

Regimental Number 69 - Robert Chancey

Robert Chancey is one Ranger who made his mark in the agricultural sector in Newfoundland. Chancey, trained at the University of British Columbia, served for a time as the Deputy Minister of Agriculture in the province and was elected to the Atlantic agriculture hall of fame in 1988.

Chancey was born August 6, 1917, in St. John's. His father was a professional golfer and his mother looked after the home. Robert completed grade eleven at Prince of Wales College, then earned a Bachelor of Science and Master of Science in Agriculture from the University of British Columbia.

After completing his schooling he worked in the field of business and commerce. He joined the Newfoundland Rangers on July 4, 1938. He served at headquarters and in quartermaster administration. His brother, Jim, was Ranger # 144.

Chancey says he joined the Rangers because it was a step up from the work he was doing. One thing he particularly remembers is training as part of the honour guard for the visit of King George V1 and Queen Elizabeth.

Robert served five years with the Rangers. He resigned from the Force to enter the Royal Canadian Navy during the Second World War. At the end of the war he took advantage of training provided to veterans to study agriculture at the University of British Columbia.

Over the years, Chancey made his mark in the field of agriculture and became director of the Brookfield Road Agricultural Research Station in St. John's. He was Deputy Minister of Agriculture, Chairman of the Avalon Consolidated School Board 1967-68, and Chairman of the School Tax Authority. He has stayed active in the Newfoundland Ranger Force Association.

Regimental Number 70 - George Sharpe

George Sharpe was a burly, stocky man and in pictures he looked as strong as a bull. Yet he died at age thirty-one while serving as a Ranger.

Sharpe was born in Whitbourne and his mother Harriet (Mercer) reared him well. His dad was a road master with the Newfoundland Railway. Sharpe got his early schooling in his hometown and finished grade eleven at Bishop Feild College.

He joined the Rangers in July 1938 and was stationed at Jackson's Arm, Glenwood, Port aux Basques, Rose Blanche and Burgeo. In 1941, he married Irene Payne and they had one son George, who later studied medicine and practiced as a doctor in Texas.

#70

Ranger Sharpe was serving at Burgeo on February 5, 1946, when he died of an aortal aneurism. His body was returned to Whitbourne for burial and laid to rest by an honour guard of Rangers.

Gordon Bennett was George Sharpe's nephew and he has fond memories of his uncle. He recalls Uncle George summoning the children to lunch by blowing loudly on a whistle.

"I can clearly remember my mother and her sister Irene, George's wife, going about the house one morning crying bitterly because he had just died," Gordon says.

#71

Regimental Number 71 - Ron Goodyear

Ronald Goodyear hailed from tiny Gooseberry Island, the son of William and Clara Goodyear. He went on to become the Chief of Police of Fredericton, New Brunswick.

He did his early schooling in Aguanthana On Newfoundland's west coast and completed grade eleven at Bishop Feild College in St. John's. He entered the Rangers around 1938 and achieved Sergeant's rank. He was posted to many detachments including Grand Bank, St. Lawrence and Burgeo.

On August 14, 1943, he married Eileen Moulton and they had four children: Ronald, Wayne, Thomas and Elizabeth.

After the Rangers were absorbed into the RCMP, Ronald transferred to that force and attained the rank of Superintendent and served as officer in charge of the Criminal Investigation Branch in St. John's, Newfoundland. When he retired from the RCMP, he served four years as the Police Chief in Fredericton, New Brunswick. Afterwards, he and his wife settled in the province.

#72

Regimental Number 72 - John Fagan

John Fagan was born in St. John's on August 2, 1919. His dad was a boiler maker with the Newfoundland Railway and his mother Johanna (Maddigan) looked after the family and home.

John completed his schooling at St. Patrick's Hall in St. John's where he finished grade eleven and a commercial course. He joined the Newfoundland Rangers on July 17, 1938, because it was the best employment option available at the time. He was posted to many detachments including Whitbourne, Deer Lake, Lewisporte, St. Lawrence, Port aux Basques, Gambo, Gander and Stephenville. John received his Sergeant's stripes while serving in Stephenville.

Fagan recalls the varied duties of a Ranger included being a wreck commissioner. In this capacity, Rangers were responsible for securing and protecting shipwrecks from looters. Fagan's commission covered Port au Port to Bay St. George.

In the early 1940s, the SS Fernfield went ashore in Picadilly Bay on Newfoundland's west coast. Fagan, accompanied by Ranger # 148, Kevin Ryan, rowed out to the wreck to keep looters away. This was dangerous work as the wreck could possibly founder. Some looters did approach but the Rangers managed to scare them off.

Ranger Fagan had many vivid memories of his time as a Ranger but rifle drill while training stood out in his mind. He also was very proud to have served in the guard of honour for the Royal visit in 1939 by the King and Queen of England. He served twelve full years as a Ranger and stayed until the force was disbanded in 1950.

Jack Fagan had a very distinguished post-Ranger career. He served as Superintendent of Her Majesty's Penitentiary and later as the province's first Director of Corrections. Fagan advocated for the need for a separate women's prison which was located in Stephenville.

After retirement, he served on the federally appointed Botterell Commission which examined seven suicides in Atlantic Canadian prisons. He has advised both politicians and judges on correctional matters. He has also been a guest speaker at the Provincial Court Judge's Association Educational Seminars.

John Fagan married schoolteacher Rita Dollard. on July 22, 1943.
The couple had one child, Maureen (Mrs. Edwin Taylor), who trained and worked as a lab technician and resides in St. John's today.

Regimental Number 73 - Lloyd Saunders

Lloyd Saunders was born in Carbonear on July 26, 1915. His father William was a cooper, his mother Ursula Clarke was a homemaker. After finishing high school in Carbonear he worked as a clerk with the Hudson's Bay Company in Labrador.

He joined the Rangers for a better career in May 1939 and was stationed at Grand Bank, Belleoram, Makkovik, Nain, Norris Arm and Badger. He stayed a Ranger for almost twelve year until the RCMP absorbed the Force.

#73

In 1946, he wed Margaret Ball and they had five children: James, William, Ursula, Evelyn and June.

Lloyd joined the Mounties in 1950 and remained with the RCMP until 1971 when he retired. He then settled in Grand Falls and became a deputy sheriff and Justice of the Peace.

#74

Regimental Number 74 - Reginald Mercer

Reginald "Reg" Mercer was born on December 26, 1920. When he died on August 12, 2002, he left behind a host of good memories with his family and friends.

Reg was the brother-in-law of Ranger # 2, Les O' Reilly. His niece, Beverly O' Reilly, says her uncle Reg was born in Whitbourne and after completing high school taught school before joining the Rangers. One of his postings was to Deer Lake where he married Bessie Glover. Together, they moved to several Ranger detachments including Meadows and Port au Port.

After leaving the Rangers, Reg joined the groundwood division with Corner Brook Pulp and Paper and worked there until he retired as groundwood supervisor. He and his wife had no children. They resided in Corner Brook until Reg's death in 2002.

Reg was a strong supporter of the Ranger Force Association and bequeathed a fairly substantial cash donation to the Ranger scholarship fund at Memorial University.

#75

Regimental Number 75 - Albert Terry

Albert Terry was born in Harbour Main on April 2, 1916. His father Michael ran a general store while his mother Mariah (Kennedy) was a homemaker.

The young Albert received his education in Harbour Main, but finished high school at St. Bonaventure's College in St. John's.

He joined the Newfoundland Ranger in May 1939 and was stationed at Gambo, Stephenville Crossing, Port aux Basques, Port au Port and Norris Arm. He served six years and six months in the Force. In the early 1940s, he was working in Baffin Island, but he retired to his home in Harbour Main because of medical problems. He passed away May 25, 1979.

Regimental Number 76 - John Parsons

#76

John Parsons was the son of Police Constable Charles Parsons and his schoolteacher wife Gertrude. His father's career always interested John and so when the opportunity arose he joined the Newfoundland Rangers.

He was well prepared for the Rangers having completed grade eleven at Prince of Wales College and further study at Memorial University College. As a Ranger, he was posted to detachments at Stephenville Crossing, Nain, Glenwood and Fortune.

In September 1941, he married Audrey Chaffey and they had four children: David, Robert, Paul and Richard.

John served six years as a Ranger and after leaving the Force worked as an accountant and manager for Clarke Steamships in Corner Brook. At the time of writing he was in relatively good health and residing at the Agnes Pratt Home in St. John's.

Regimental Number 77 - Arthur Morris

#77

Arthur "Art" Morris was the son of sea captain Fred Morris and his wife Georgina. He was raised in the family home in Sandy Point. Art was born December 1920 and educated at Sandy Point and St. George's on the west coast.

After completing high school, he entered the Rangers in 1941. He remained a Ranger until they were absorbed by the RCMP in 1950. Art earned the rank of Corporal and had postings to Port aux Basques, Belleoram, Grand Bank, Deer Lake, Stephenville, and Goose Bay.

In 1953, he wed Rosemary Jordan and they had four children: Margaret, Bonita, Thomas and Susan. He retired with the rank of Staff Sgt. and settled in Ottawa, Ontario.

Regimental Number 78 - John Channing

John Channing was born in St. John's in March 1920. His father, John, was a shoemaker, and his mother, Mary (Saunders), was a homemaker. John was educated at St. Patrick's Hall in St. John's where he earned grade eleven. He joined the Rangers in 1941 and stayed for two years eight months. He was posted to St. George's, Burin, Codroy, Hopedale, and the training depot. He later settled in Montreal and went to sea as a merchant sailor.

#79

Regimental Number 79 - John Hogan

John Hogan is surely one of the most well known Newfoundland Rangers. His near death adventure on Newfoundland's Northern Peninsula has been the subject of many newspaper articles and Horwood devoted chapter 15 in his History of the Ranger Force to Hogan's story.

Hogan was born in Carbonear in 1910 to James, a butcher, and Catherine (Doody). Prior to entering the Rangers, Hogan attended Memorial University College and taught school for nine years on the Northern Peninsula. But he left the classroom and chalk board behind for the rugged, adventure of the Rangers.

He joined the Rangers February 10, 1941, and was posted to detachments in Bay L'Argent, Gander, Goose Bay and Deer Lake.

While stationed at Goose Bay in 1943, Hogan was due to go on leave and on May 8th was offered a flight on an Air Force plane going to Gander. While in the air, the plane filled with smoke and when the pilot went into a dive to flush the smoke out, Hogan and two airmen leapt from the plane using parachutes. It was little they knew of the ordeal they were about to experience.

The men parachuted onto the rugged Northern Peninsula near Hawke's Bay. Hogan kept himself and one of the injured airman alive until they were rescued in late June. He provided food for the pair by catching rabbits and picking berries. For his valour, Hogan was awarded the King's Police and Fire Service Medal and he was promoted to Corporal.

He married Eudora Billiard and they had two children, Bernadette and Helena. Eudora and Bernadette drowned while traveling from Castor River to Port aux Choix on April 16, 1938. Helena was later killed in a motor vehicle accident.

Hogan married for a second time, wedding Margaret O'Flaherty on February 20, 1944. They had three children: Rosemary, Maureen and Kevin. The two girls have distinguished themselves as teachers, while Kevin has made his mark in the health care field. Kevin is currently a staff psychiatrist at the Waterford Hospital and has served as Assistant Deputy Minister of Health and Medical Director at the Janeway Children's Hospital.

John Hogan's youngest grand-daughter is a medical doctor and the 2004 Newfoundland Rhodes Scholar.

Despite his near death mishap, Hogan remained in the Rangers until it was absorbed into the RCMP. Hogan joined the Mounties and attained the rank of Staff Sergeant. He retired to pension from the RCMP in 1966 and went to work with the National Harbour Board in St. John's. He died on April 20, 1977, just one day after retiring from the Harbour Board.

Contributor Robert Smith recalls John Hogan's name coming up among a group of middle aged men in Deer Lake some 50 years after Hogan's service there. One man was succinct in his summary: "Hogan was tough but fair," he said. "Few would challenge him and those few who did regretted the challenge."

A mountain on the rugged Northern Peninsula has been named Mount Hogan in his honor.

Regimental Number 80 - Nathan Penney

#80

Nathan Penney was born November 28, 1920, in St. John's. His parents were Frank and Mabel (Taylor) Penney. Nathan was educated at Centenary Hall School and then at Holloway School and Prince of Wales Collegiate.

Prior to joining the Rangers in May, 1941, he worked in his father's business, Frank Penney Trading Company.

Nathan Penney recalls why he joined the Rangers. "I was encouraged to join and had a favorable impression of the Rangers from Ed Martin (Reg. No. 10), a neighbor on LeMarchant Road. He provided me with an application form."

Penney served five years with the Rangers and left when his contract expired in 1946. Later that year he married Grace Leavey and they had two children Mavis and Frank.

After leaving the Rangers, Nathan worked in the family business. Following his retirement, he and his wife settled in Masonic Park in Mount Pearl, Newfoundland.

Regimental Number 81 - Edward Hudson

#81

Born in Blackhead, Bay de Verde, on August 1921, Edward Hudson joined the Rangers in May 1941. His father Douglas had been a schoolteacher while his mother Lillian (Moores) was a homemaker. Edward had completed grade eleven prior to joining the Rangers. He served for a relatively short period between six and twelve months.

In September 1944, he married Chrissie (Crawley) and they had two children, Douglas and Joan. The couple settled in Blackhead where they owned and operated a confectionary store and gas bar.

Regimental Number 82 - Michael Hogan

#82

Michael Hogan was born in Northern Bay in June 1916. His dad Francis was a fisherman, his mother Bridgett (Howell) was a homemaker. He completed grade eleven in Northern Bay and joined the Rangers in May 1941. He served as a Ranger for only a brief period, for less than one year. He was a Supernumerary, stationed in Gander.

He wed Mary O'Dwyer in 1945 and they settled in Stephenville Crossing where he operated a thriving wholesale business. They had a large family: Andrew, James, Martina, Veronica, Gordon, Pius, Paul, John, and Sharon.

Regimental Number 83 - John MacDonald

John Clarence MacDonald was born in St. John's on December 20, 1920. His father John was a physician, his mother Ellen (Moore) a housewife.

John was educated at St. Bon's where he earned grade eleven. He joined the Rangers in May 1941 as a Supernumerary or special Constable. He served for less than six months in Gander.

He wed Rose (Loverde) and they had one son, Michael John. They settled in Seminole, Florida.

John worked in the media with VONF radio in St. John's and at WHEC radio in Rochester, New

#83

York. He made a major career change later in life. On October 16, 1989, at age 69, he was ordained a priest. Sadly, serious medical problems followed and he died on March 28, 1990.

Regimental Number 84 - Vincent Noonan

Vincent Noonan was a Ranger and latterly a member of the Newfoundland Constabulary. He was born in Northern Bay, Conception Bay, on January 16, 1919. His father Edward was a miner and fisherman, while his mother Mary (nee Lynch) was a housewife.

After finishing high school in Northern Bay, Vincent worked in a fish liver factory. But the lure of the Rangers varied work was too much to resist and so young Vincent joined the Rangers in May 1941. No doubt the upward employment mobility also attracted him to the position.

#84

Vincent was one of a group of Rangers known as a "Supernumerary," or special duty Ranger. These men were under the command of the Ranger-in-Charge of the Gander Detachment at the time.

In this capacity he gained valuable experience in police work that no doubt helped him earn his way into the Newfoundland Constabulary in 1942.

He served as a member of the mounted division of the Constabulary until its disbandment in 1951. At the time of his death, he was the last surviving member of the initial Constabulary Mounted Unit. Following retirement from the police force, he was employed as a car salesman with Terra Nova Motors.

#85

Regimental Number 85 - Gerald Doyle

Gerald Doyle (born October 22, 1921) was from Bay de Verde, Gull Island. His father William operated a grocery store while his mother Ellen (English) looked after the home and family.

Gerald was educated in Northern Bay and earned his high school diploma there. Like Vincent Noonan, he joined the Rangers in May 1941 as a Supernumerary and was stationed at Gander for approximately six to twelve months.

On April 22, 1943, he enlisted in the Newfoundland Constabulary and remained with that Force until 1947.

In 1945, he married Thersea (Penney) and they had four daughters: Geraldine, Shirley, Helen, Linda.

After leaving the Constabulary, he was employed doing security work at the U.S. Harmon airbase in Stephenville. Sadly, he met death by drowning at the early age of 32.

#86

Regimental Number 86 - Ephriam Tucker

Ephriam Tucker was born in Burnt Point on April 8, 1916. His father Jordan was a fisherman, while his mother Gertrude (Oliver) looked after the home and family. He earned grade eleven in Burnt Point and then worked alongside his father as a small boat fisherman.

He joined the Rangers in May 1941 and was posted to Gander for special duty in June of that year. He served approximately six months as a Supernumerary Ranger.

The year 1941 was a busy one for Ephriam. He married Mildred (Wicks) in June. The couple had six children: Cyril, Gwendolyn, Marilyn, Hayward (Derek), Armorel and Valerie.

He raised and supported his family by working as a carpenter in the Topsail area where he settled.

Regimental Number 87 - Francis Hannon

#87

Francis "Frank" Hannon hailed from the town of Harbour Main, Conception Bay. He was born on April 9, 1917, to a schoolteacher father, Patrick, and a stay-at-home mother, Agnes.

After finishing high school in Harbour Main, Frank joined the Rangers as a Supernumerary because it was a "good job" and promised adventure. His wife, Madonna (Coady), recalls that Frank often talked of his adventures in the Rangers, in which he served nine years 71 days. He was posted to Gander, Bay L'Argent, Hermitage, Gambo, Petite Forte and Marystown. His brother Gerald was Ranger # 93.

Frank stayed with the Rangers until the Force was disbanded in 1950 and he took a transfer to the RCMP where he remained until retirement.

He married in 1949 and he and his wife had three children: Regina (deceased); Kevin and Martina.

Regimental Number 88 - Graham Percy

Graham Percy was a fisherman and the son of a fisherman. He was born March 12, 1916, to Frederick and Greta (Spracklin) of Brigus. After finishing high school he worked with his father in the fishing industry.

He joined the Rangers in May 1941 as a Supernumerary, or special duty Ranger. He was posted to Gander in June of that year. The Rangers offered good employment opportunities and a way forward for the educated young man.

In a letter dated December 15,1941, Acting

#88

Chief Ranger R.D. Fraser discussed Percy's Ranger service as "trustworthy and reliable." He was given an honorable discharge after six months on the expiration of his contract.

He married Blanche (Youden) in April 1946, and they had four children: Roy, Winston, Chris and Jacqueline. He supported his family by working as a Rigger at the U.S. Naval base in Argentia. After retiring in 1977, he settled in Brigus.

#89

Regimental Number 89 - Thomas Kane

Thomas Kane was another one of the Supernumeraries, or special duty Rangers. He joined the Force in May 1941 and stayed for six to twelve months.

The son of Thomas and Elizabeth Kane of Conception Harbour earned his grade eleven diploma in that town.

After leaving the Rangers, Thomas worked as a blacksmith in Conception Harbour. He married Mary Dalton in 1949 and they had two children, Paul and Elizabeth.

#90

Regimental Number 90 - James Foley

James "Jim" Foley was born in St. John's on October 6, 1918. His father Patrick was a manager with Royal Stores, his mother Bride (Careen) a homemaker.

Jim finished high school at St. Bon's and worked as a clerk with James Baird Company. He joined the Rangers in May 1941 as a Supernumerary member, or special duty member. He was posted to Gander and served less than one year. He later told his brother of long, lonely nights spent patrolling Gander Lake in a small boat related to his security duties.

He later married Frances Foley and they had three children: Frances, Gregory and Bernard.

The couple settled in Niagara Falls, and Jim worked with the Provincial Government of Ontario as head contractor, a job he obtained because of his background in construction.

Regimental Number 91 - Dudley Crowther

Dudley Crowther experienced the Second World War first hand when a German U-boat sank an allied ship off the coast of Labrador and the survivors ended up billeted with Ranger Crowther.

Dudley was born in St. John's on June 18, 1919. He attended Prince of Wales College and finished grade eleven there.

He joined the Rangers in 1941 and was stationed in Stephenville, Battle Harbour, Harbour Breton, Pushthrough and Fortune.

#91

Dudley married Beatrice Snooks in June 1942 and they had eight children. He remained a Ranger until 1950 at which time he joined the RCMP. He retired from that Force in 1963 and went to work as chief of security for Wabush Mines in Labrador, a position he held until 1980.

During the summer of 1942, Dudley was stationed in Battle Harbour, Labrador, when an allied convoy en route to Goose Bay and Greenland was attacked by a Nazi sub. The U-boat sank the SS Chatham and one hundred and sixty survivors came ashore in Battle Harbour. Three men were badly burned and Crowther took them to the Grenfell Mission in Mary's Harbour. The others he put up in the school and supplied them with food and sleeping gear from the local merchant. After a week, an American warship came to pick up the survivors. Crowther received a commendation from both the U.S. Navy and the Chief Ranger for his actions. He retired in St. John's where he died in October 2005.

Regimental Number 92 - J. Butt

This man was only in the Ranger Force for two days. He was discharged on the second day of his enlistment after it was discovered he had tuberculosis. Sadly, it is believed he died shortly after being discharged.

Regimental Number 93 - Gerald Hannon

#93

Gerald Hannon served as both a Supernumerary Ranger and a regular duty Ranger at two separate times, serving a total of four years.

He was born in Harbour Main on August 15, 1923. His father Patrick was a teacher, in fact Gerald completed high school under the tutoring of his father. His mother Agnes looked after the family home.

Prior to becoming a Supernumerary, Gerald worked as a time-keeper on the U.S. base at Argentia. But he joined the Rangers in 1941 and served for six months in Gander. He later rejoined the Rangers as a regular duty member in 1944 and was stationed at Battle Harbour, St. George's, Meadows Point and Hebron.

Gerald left the Rangers in September 1947 and married Grace Cleary in 1955. They had one son, Patrick, a chemistry teacher at Memorial University.

From 1951 to 1972, Gerald was a member of the Canadian Army Signal Corps. After retiring from this branch of the services, he settled in his hometown of Harbour Main.

Regimental Number 94 - Roland Caines

#94

Roland was the son of fisherman/merchant George Caines and his wife Melissa (Reid). He was born in Norris Point on July 12, 1906, and earned grade eleven there.

Roland applied for the Ranger Force in 1935, but for reasons unknown he instead went to work in the Turks Island in the West Indies where he was manager of a salt processing plant. He returned to Newfoundland in 1941 and joined the Ranger Force. He was posted to Hebron, but in 1942 was transferred to Antilak Bay, Nain, to operate a sawmill under the Northern Labrador Administration (NLA)

In May 1943, he took a discharge from the Rangers and later that same year married Lulu (Hicks). They had five children: Patricia (deceased), Edith and Judith (twins), Elizabeth, Susan (deceased). His brother Cliff was Ranger # 111.

From 1943 to 1947, Roland managed government trading depots at Davis Inlet and Hebron under the NLA. He left Hebron in 1949 and returned to Norris Point where he owned a general store. He eventually settled in Cambridge, Ontario.

Regimental Number 95 - Norman Crane

#95

Norman Crane has been the driving force behind the Newfoundland Ranger Force Association since its inception. He was born in St. John's to John and Salome (Parker) Crane. Norman was educated at Bishop Feild College where he completed grade eleven and a commercial course.

Prior to enlisting in the Rangers, he was employed as an office clerk for the Newfoundland Division of the Canadian National Institute for the Blind.

He joined the Rangers in July 1941 looking for adventure. A chance encounter with Dudley Crowther, Ranger # 91, who told him about an outport police force led Norman to join the Force. Crane found adventure in the many places he was posted including Port Aux Basques, Codroy Valley, Glenwood, Springdale and Bay L'Argent. He served five full years as a Ranger and left the Force with an honourable discharge in September 1946.

In 1951, he married Penelope Goodridge and they had a large family of six children: Joan, Janet, Andrew, Daphne, Marion and James.

After leaving the Rangers, Norman worked with the Provincial Department of Health and Welfare, including involvement with the Cottage Hospital system and the management of sanatoriums in Corner Brook and St. John's. Eventually he found his way into employment with Johnson and Johnson Ltd. as a salesman and area manager. He stayed in this position for 35 years and was elected to the Johnson and Johnson Sales Hall of Fame.

Norman had a variety of exciting and interesting experiences while a Ranger. For example, the SS Caribou was torpedoed while he was stationed in the Codroy Valley and he aided in the recovery of bodies.

While stationed in Glenwood, he had the grisly task of burying the corpse of Esau Gillingham, a trapper and woodsman known for his role in Horwood's story "White Eskimo." At one point prior to his death, Gillingham got into a confrontation with a railroad agent over missing liquor. Crane had to disarm Gillingham and find the missing hooch. The armed stand-off was settled quietly and without charges being laid.

Some time later, Gillingham went missing on the headwaters of the Gander River. Crane and a search party found the partly decomposed body on the banks of the river. It was later determined he died of natural causes. Crane saw to the burial of the body and read the "Rite of Burial" over the corpse.

Crane also helped deliver a baby in a cabin boat between St. Bernard's and Bay L'Argent. This case was mentioned in Horwood's History of the Ranger Force.

Norman Crane (along with Ches Parsons # 152) was heavily involved with this book's publication. There were many meetings held at Norm's house to plan and discuss the book. Norm played a particularly crucial role in the collection of photos.

Regimental Number 96 - Albert Mews

#96

Albert "Bert" Mews was born in St. John's on August 13, 1917. His father Ashton was in the grocery business, his mother Julia a homemaker. He completed grade eleven at Prince of Wales College and worked as a salesman for a period.

He joined the Rangers in 1941 because of his love of the rugged outdoor lifestyle led by the Rangers.

Upon leaving the Force he was officially commended by Major Fraser, Chief Ranger, for his excellent plainclothes work in the Deer Lake area which led to prosecutions under the Alcoholic Liquors Act.

He never married and worked with the Provincial Government of Newfoundland until his retirement.

Regimental Number 97 - John Luscombe

#97

John "Jack" Luscombe was born in St. John's on November 8, 1921. His father, John Luscombe, was an accountant with the Auditor General of Newfoundland and was made a Member of the British Empire in 1948. His mother Claire (Gardiner) was a school teacher.

Jack attended school at Prince of Wales College and earned grade eleven there. He joined the Rangers in 1941 and served a total of seven years. He was posted to detachments in

Twillingate, Burgeo, Grand Bank, St. Lawrence, Port aux Basques, Rose Blanche, Badger, Goose Bay, Gambo and Meadow's Point.

The promise of adventure, a new challenge and a very different lifestyle helped attract Jack to the Rangers, especially after he was turned down for military service by the Royal Artillery.

A year before he left the Rangers he married nurse Evelyn Sheppard. They had three children, Sylvia, Nancy and John.

While still in the Rangers he helped recover bodies of victims from the ill-fated SS Caribou. Jack recalls "The recovery of bodies of friends and acquaintances, of crew members wearing their uniforms and the stewardess wearing a crew members jacket, as well as the responsibility of identifying the body of a relative had a very profound and lasting effect."

Luscombe almost died while on Ranger duty. It happened while he and Ranger # 123, Jim Bragg, were stationed on the south coast. A very frantic man ran up to the Rangers and informed them that a boat loaded with explosives was on fire in the harbour. The two Rangers ran down to the harbour and set the burning boat adrift so that the explosion would occur offshore. Only when the boat had drifted out a ways did the Rangers learn from one of the gathered crowd that there was a man on board. The two Rangers bravely boarded a dory and rowed out to the burning vessel. Jack Luscombe held the smaller boat steady while Jim Bragg hopped aboard the burning vessel and carried the injured man back to the dory. The two Rangers rowed frantically away from the foundering ship when a loud explosion showered them with debris. Luckily they were far enough from the ship to be spared death or injury. Luscombe and Bragg remained life-long friends after that near death event.

After leaving the Rangers in 1948, Jack moved to Toronto, Ontario, where he was employed with the Canadian Pacific Railway Police. He advanced through the ranks to become an investigator and retired form the force at sixty years of age. He retired in Gravenhurst, Ontario.

On May 20, 1984, he was awarded the Police Exemplary Service Medal in recognition of thirty years of loyal police service in Canada.

#98

Regimental Number 98 - Dorman Foster

Dorman "Dorm" was both a Ranger and an RCMP member. He was a policeman at heart.

He was born in LaScie in November 1917. His father John was a fisherman, while his mother Winnifred (Burton) was a homemaker.

Dorm completed grade eleven in LaScie and was employed as a schoolteacher after leaving school. However, dusty chaulk boards and spelling books were not for him. He joined the Newfoundland Rangers on August 14, 1941.

During his nine years as a Ranger, he earned the rank of Corporal and saw postings to Gander, Petit Forte, Meadows Point, St. Lawrence and Stephenville Crossing.

On July 6, 1946, he married Clara (Bavis). Together they had six children: Wayne, William, Elizabeth (Beth), Eugene, Susan and Darrin. His daughter, Beth Marshall, was elected as MHA for Topsail District in the 2003 provincial general election.

In 1950, when the RCMP absorbed the Rangers, Dorm became a Mountie. Thirty years later he retired with the rank of Staff Sergeant.

On July 28, 1968, Dorm published a history of the Ranger Force in the Grand Falls Advertiser.

The following is a quote from that publication: In continuing to grow and expand, the Force gradually began to build a reputation around itself and in most areas the Rangers were the only representatives of government and many requests were made of their services, some of which would require the wisdom of Solomon to solve. Many residents in the rural areas, most of whom were honest, hardworking fishermen, loggers or farmers liked nothing better than to be met on the fish flakes or stages, in the fields or woods during the morning and wished the time of day by an almost complete stranger, who at times addressed them as Aunt Mary or Uncle John. In later years, many residents often referred to members as "My or our Ranger" and on one occasion, a young boy, seeing a member approach for the first time, said "Dad, look at the strange man coming up the road." And the reply was, "Son, that is not a man, that is a Ranger."

Dorm later worked as chief of security with Abitibi Price at the Grand Falls Pulp and Paper Mill. He died December 1, 1980.

Regimental Number 99 - Ralph Janes

Ralph was born September 23, 1916, in Black Head, Broad Cove. His mother, Jane (Budgell), was a homemaker. His father, William, was a sales merchant.

He completed his schooling in Black Head and after obtaining grade eleven taught school in the White Bay area.

He joined the Rangers in August 1941 and served for one year and eight months. He was stationed at Howley and on a patrol boat along the coast. He left the Rangers in April 1943.

#99

He then served in the Royal Newfoundland Regiment, another Ranger who felt the call of patriotism during wartime. He was later employed with the federal Department of Public Works at St. John's airport. He retired in the mid-1970s. Ralph married Millicent Moores in 1950 and they had one child, Bernice. Ralph passed away on January 21, 2003.

Regimental Number 100 - Allan Garfield Anstey

Allan Anstey had a long, varied law enforcement career. He went from being a Ranger to a RCMP Staff Sergeant to being a provincial Magistrate.

Anstey was born in the central Newfoundland town of Springdale on March 2, 1920. His father Frederick worked in the lumber woods, while his mother Mary Ann (Jenkins) was a homemaker.

Allan completed grade eleven in Springdale and was employed doing survey work. He joined the Newfoundland Rangers in August 1941 at the age of 21. He remained a Ranger for almost nine

#100

years until the force was absorbed into the Mounties. By 1950, Anstey had risen to the rank of Corporal.

He married Verna Torraville in January 1954 and they had four children- Frederick, Robert, Carol Ann and Peter.

He retired from the RCMP on May 1, 1967, and was immediately engaged as a Provincial Magistrate. He retired from this post on March 31 and settled in Gander.

#101

Regimental Number 101 - Douglas Lloyd Small

Douglas Lloyd Small had an interesting life for sure. After serving as a Ranger, he helped set up municipal government in Summerford and served as Mayor of the town.

He was born on January 18, 1917, and passed away on March 19, 1990. His mother Venetta Wheeler was a housewife while his father Martin ran a sawmill. He completed grade eleven at Summerford School and after finishing his education he taught school for four years. He joined the Rangers in 1941 on the encouragement of local Magistrate Abbott.

Douglas saw postings to many detachments including Whitbourne, Gander, St. Anthony, Grand Bank, Belleoram, Port aux Port and Stephenville.

While stationed in Port au Port, he was forced to draw his service revolver and fire at a fleeing suspect. Douglas intentionally missed the suspect and shot only to scare him. The tactic worked and the man stopped his flight upon hearing the gunshot.

In 1947, he married schoolteacher Nellie Powell from Happy Adventure. The couple had two sons, Douglas Frederick and Martin James.

Douglas served 7-1/2 years in the Ranger Force before receiving an honourable discharge in 1949. He then worked as a sawmill operator in Summerford. The firm of M.J. Small and Sons is still in operation today and is managed by his son Douglas.

Upon his death in 1990, the then Mayor of Summerford, Wayne Jenkins, wrote a tribute to Douglas Small in the local paper, noting he was active in the Orange Lodge, the outport development association, The Notre Dame Hospital Board, the volunteer fire hall and the local church.

No doubt Summerford was proud to call Douglas Small a native son.

Regimental Number 102 - Bert Tilley

Bert Tilley was born in Elliston, Trinity Bay, on April 9, 1915. His father Marmaduke was a fisherman/farmer, while his mother Emily (Pearce) was a school teacher. Bert was educated in Elliston and completed grade eleven there.

He joined the Rangers between July and September 1941 and was posted to Port Saunders and Nain. He served his five year hitch before departing the Force. His brother Bob was also a Ranger # 112.

#102

He wed Ethel Baker on August 27, 1940, something which makes him the only recruit to be married when he entered the Ranger Force.

After leaving the Rangers he owned and operated a grocery store at Elliston and later worked as an accountant for Bowaters at Hawke's Bay. He eventually settled in St. John's.

Regimental Number 103 - George Pauls

George Pauls holds the distinction of being the youngest man to join the Rangers.

He was born in St. Jacques, Fortune Bay, on February 16, 1925. His father George Sr. was a sea-cook, his mother Emily (nee Saint) a nurse.

George earned his grade eleven at the Convent School in St. Jacques. He joined the Rangers in May 1942. George was only seventeen and while men were supposed to be nineteen to join the Rangers, he somehow managed to get in. No doubt he was the youngest Ranger!

#103

George says one of the main reasons he joined the Rangers was that he found the idea of enforcing the game laws very appealing. He has fond memories of Ranger training and the close friendships forged there.

As a Ranger, George was stationed at Goose Bay, Hopedale and Grand Bank. He served a little over three years before being honorably discharged.

While stationed in Hopedale in July 1944 he was ordered by headquarters to be on the look-out for a German submarine reported to be in the area. Sometime after the end of hostilities it was determined that the German Navy had indeed gone ashore on the Labrador and set up weather forecasting equipment to aid its operations.

George Pauls was mentioned in a letter from United States President Roosevelt to Church of England Clergyman Parson Clench regarding Pauls' involvement in the recovery and internment of the body of a U.S. sailor from the USS Pollux which ran aground on the Burin Peninsula.

George Pauls was twice married and had five children: Elaine (Mrs. Wayne Turpin), Eleanor (deceased), Bernadine (Mrs. Dan Shipley), Mary (Mrs. Don Oakley) and RNC Sgt. George Jr.

After leaving the Rangers, George Pauls led an interesting life. He served as a policeman in both the Vancouver City Police Force and the Ontario Provincial Police. He also worked as a detective for the Civil Aviation Division of the Newfoundland Government.

Today, George Pauls lives in Nova Scotia but remains very active in the Newfoundland Ranger Force Association and played a large role in the creation of this book. He was a wealth of information on deceased members of the Force and had a large collection of relevant photos.

#104

Regimental Number 104 - William Keeping

William "Bill" Keeping was born in Grand Bank on September 2, 1923. His father John was a cook, his mother Mary Ann a homemaker. Bill finished high school in Grand Bank and then completed teacher's training. He joined the Rangers in 1942, but served less than six months and was never posted to detachment.

In 1945, he married Mabel Williams and they had three children: Bill, Doreen and Derek. He owned and operated his own insurance company, Merit Insurance. He also served as Governor of the Kiwanis Club.

Regimental Number 105 - Jack LaFosse

Jack LaFosse says that when he was a young man in school the local Ranger in Belleoram was such a good example and role model. that he was inspired to become a Ranger himself.

Jack was born in New Harbour, Hermitage Bay. This little town later became Parsons Harbour. Jack's father was John, a fisherman, and his mom Maggie was a housewife.

He started school in New Harbour and finished grade eleven in Belleoram. After completing high school he did some teacher training and taught for one year before entering the Rangers.

Jack joined the Rangers in May 1942 and was posted to Whitbourne for training. He served at detachments in Deer Lake, Badger, the training depot, and Quarter Master Stores at Kilbride. He was wed in August 1947 to Louise Jacobs and they had two children; Cheryl and Darrell.

He served a total of seven years as a Ranger, becoming a Mountie in 1950 when the RCMP took over policing duties for the province. He was with the RCMP until 1977, a total of 35 years of service. Jack retired from the RCMP with the commissioned rank of Superintendent. His daughter Cheryl is an RCMP member and was one of the first women engaged in the Force in Newfoundland. His son is presently an Assistant RCMP Commissioner in Ottawa.

Jack says while he has many, many stories of his Ranger days "none are particularly fascinating to anyone but myself."

Regimental Number 106 - Arthur Pratt

Arthur "Art" Pratt was born October 15, 1922, in St. John's. His father was James, his mother, Minnie (Kerr). Art completed grade eleven at Prince of Wales College and joined the Rangers in May 1942. He served for almost two years.

In 1947, he wed Minnie Parsons and they had two sons: Douglas and Gerald. The family settled in St. John's where Art worked at newspaper and public relations work.

#106

Regimental Number 107 - Eric Bruce Gillingham

Eric "Bruce" Gillingham had a long varied career which included time as a Ranger, a RCMP officer and a Superintendent with Newfoundland Hydro. While serving as a Ranger he was decorated for disarming a rifle-wielding killer.

Gillingham was born in St. John's on April 28, 1923, to Harold, a contractor, and Maude, a homemaker. He was educated at Holloway and Prince of Wales College and joined the Rangers on May 21,1942.

While a Ranger, he saw postings to Hebron, St. Lawrence, Grand Bank, Burin, Port Aux Basques and Norris Arm. Bruce Gillingham saw his share of exciting and dangerous adventures.

#107

During the month of April 1943, while stationed at Hebron, the most northerly Ranger post in Labrador, Bruce was the first government representative to visit the site of a U.S. airplane crash at Saglek.

The plane had crashed in December 1942 with seven people on board. Gillingham found four people huddled together in the wreckage, dead from starvation. A diary indicated that three others were attempting to row to Goose Bay in a rubber dinghy, but they were never heard from afterwards.

On October 23, 1948, Bruce was almost killed on duty by a suspect who fired a gun at him. The suspect had no intention of letting Gillingham take him in. He shot at Gillingham but the bullet passed under his right arm, just missing his ribs.

Gillingham disarmed the man and arrested him and he was convicted of murder. Gillingham could have shot the man with his revolver but chose instead to risk his own life by capturing him. For his courageous actions Gillingham was awarded the King's Police and Fire Services medal on September 1, 1949.

A footnote to the story is that many years later, after Bruce retired from the RCMP and was superintendent with the Bishop's Falls division of Newfoundland Hydro, the man who tried to kill him was employed under his command at Hydro. This was after he had completed his prison term. The story reflects Gillingham's humanity and ability to live and let live.

In March 1949, the same year he was decorated, Bruce married Beryl Poole. They had four children: Shirley, Craig, Anne and Edward.

Regimental Number 108 - Charles Goulding

#108

The most memorable thing Charles Goulding recalls about Ranger training is the get togethers at barracks in Whitbourne. But his most vivid memory of being a Ranger is how very sad he felt when he was completing applications for the dole (relief). The sadness he felt in dealing with impoverished people led him to leave the Rangers after about a year's service.

Charles was born in 1922 in Grand Falls. His father Garfield worked at the Anglo-Newfoundland Development Co. paper mill in Grand Falls, while his mom Isabella looked after the home and family.

He completed grade eleven in his hometown and joined the Rangers in

1942. He was stationed in Bonne Bay and Norris Point. But he left after completing about a year's service.

He married Frances Mayne in November 1948 and they had four children: Cheryl, Eunice, Jean and Marilyn.

After leaving the Rangers he went to work as a paymaster for Bowaters Paper Company in Howley. He moved to Toronto in 1957 and worked in accounting until his retirement in 1987. His brother Nelson was Ranger # 43.

Regimental Number 109 - Archibald White

Archibald "Arch" White was born in St. John's on December 22, 1921. He was a twin, his brother being John White who went on to be a magistrate and author.

#109

Arch's father Stanley was an insurance agent, his mother Charlotte (Knight) a homemaker. Arch finished grade eleven at Prince of Wales College and then worked as an accountant.

He joined the Rangers in August 1942 and served almost two years. He later married Maisie Coffin and they had five children: George, Ronald, Sharon, Audrey, Larry.

Arch worked at Argentia and later was the paymaster at the Iron Ore Company of Canada in Shefferville from 1960 - 1980. He retired to Carbonear.

Regimental Number 110 - Ian King

Ian King completed pre-Medicine at Memorial University College and was supposed to go to Med School on a four year scholarship but was side-tracked by a trip to the sanatorium with tuberculosis.

#110

Ian was born August 27, 1923, at 20 Charlton Street in St. John's. His father was Alfred who ran a grocery store at 128 Casey Street, but later designed and built fine homes. His mother was a seamstress and ran the grocery after Alfred's death.

Ian earned his grade eleven and grade eleven commercial at Prince of Wales College prior to attending Memorial University College .He completed a year of pre-medicine before getting sick.

Prior to joining the Rangers he worked as a customs clerk with White Clothing Company and Crane Ltd. He officially enlisted in the Rangers on May 28, 1942. He was first stationed in Stephenville Crossing and later in Forteau, Labrador.

Ian was "recruited" into the Rangers by Ranger # 97 Jack Luscombe, who was from Casey Street and knew the King family.

Ian left the Rangers in May, 1945. He was "granted discharge by purchase at his own request in order to continue his educational studies."

In July 1952, he married Ethelwynne Winsor in Wesley United Church in St. John's. Ethelwynne's father was a Minister and he performed the marriage ceremony. The couple had four children: Derrick, Dianne, Graham and Lynda.

The couple relocated to the Vancouver area in 1957 and he worked in health agency management for many years. He later entered the field of consulting, creating his own consulting firm in 1980.

Ian says he had a relatively quiet time as a Ranger and his most memorable case involved an arsonist's repeated attempts to burn down the school in Codroy Valley. King staked out the school occasionally but the arsonist finally succeeded in burning it to the ground.

King recalls that Sgt. Bill Smith (Ranger # 56 and father of co-author Robert Smith) came out from St. George's to aid in the investigation. The two Rangers could not determine who the firebug was. But King says he has good memories of working with Smith. King has recounted his entire life in an unpublished biography.

Regimental Number 111 - Clifford Caines

#111

Clifford Caines was born in Norris Point on March 28, 1922. His father George was a fisherman while his mother Melissa (Reid) looked after the home and family.

Clifford earned grade eleven at Norris Point School and then followed his brother Roland Caines (# 94) and joined the Ranger Force sometime between December 1941 and June 1942. The length of his service and his discharge date are not known. His son Paul is of the opinion that his dad purchased his way out of the five year Ranger contract.

In 1947, Clifford married Gertrude (Whiteway) and they had four sons: Paul, Derek, Brian and Blair. By this time Clifford was employed with Bowaters Paper Company, first as a scaler, later as a Safety Inspector in the woods department. The couple made their home in Corner Brook.

Regimental Number 112 - Robert Tilley

Robert Tilley may have been drawn into the Ranger Force by his brother Bert (# 102) who joined earlier. Robert was born in Elliston on June 11, 1922. He was educated at Elliston school and at Memorial University College. He worked as a school teacher prior to joining the Rangers.

#112

He entered the Rangers in June 1942 and was stationed at Codroy, Burgeo, Lewisporte and Port Saunders. He served for five years and was honorably discharged on June 3, 1947.

Robert married Mary Badcock in 1947 and they had six children: Catherine, Robert, Patricia, Susan, Gregory and Anne.

The couple settled in St. John's and Robert supported the large family by working as a salesman. He was also an agent for Crown Life Insurance.

Regimental Number 113 - Austin Vardy

Austin Vardy was the son of WWI veteran, Reuben T. Vardy, and Amelia (Maddock). The couple ran a general store and Reuben also fished and logged. Austin was schooled in Hickman's Harbour and at Bond Street School in St. John's. Prior to joining the Rangers, Austin worked in the family business on Random Island.

He joined the Rangers in 1942 and was stationed in Kilbride and Goose Bay, Labrador. Austin was interested in social welfare and keeping the peace and so Ranger service attracted him.

While a Ranger, Austin got frostbitten while sleeping in a tent and was hospitalized as a result. He lost a toe and part of his foot at that time. He was discharged shortly after this event.

After the end of the Second World War, he married Clara Roberts of Twillingate. The couple had three children: Donna, Darlene and Gerald. Austin later took the family to Toronto where he worked as a salesman for Morgan Paper Company.

Austin died in 2001, and both he and his wife are buried in the family plot in Hickman's Harbour, his birthplace.

Regimental Number 114 - Don Patey

#114

You might say that Don Patey had a lot of ups and down after he left the Rangers. You see he was a commercial pilot.

Don came from St. Anthony where he was born on May 28, 1921. His parents were Arthur and Jessie Patey. Don was educated in St. Anthony at Grenfell Amalgamated and joined the Ranger Force in June 1942. He was posted to Stephenville, Goose Bay and Battle Harbour. The outdoor lifestyle of the Rangers attracted Don to the force. But he only stayed with the force for two years. Don says that he can still remember transporting a prisoner by train from St. George's to St. John's. "The print of the old wooden seats in second class is probably still in my rear end," he says.

In 1953 he married Margaret King, and they had four children: Leonard, Donna, Janine and Arlene. Don supported his family by working as a commercial pilot in Newfoundland, Ontario and Quebec.

Don's daughter, Donna, joined the RCMP in 1981 and is serving in British Columbia today.

Regimental Number 115 - Malcolm Squires

#115

Malcolm Squires was not only a Ranger but also the superintendent of her Majesty's Penitentiary (HMP). and a past master of the St. John's Masonic Lodge. To say he led a full life is an understatement.

He was born in St. Phillips on February 17, 1917, one of seven children of Daisy and William Squires. Malcolm completed grades one to ten in a one room school in St. Phillips and finished grade eleven at Bishop Feild College. He also attended Memorial University College.

Squires was employed as a teacher from 1935-1941. He taught in one room schools in Labrador and on the island. In 1941, he joined the Newfoundland Constabulary's Criminal Investigation Division and while serving in that capacity he met the chief Ranger.

Squires asked about the Ranger Force and was attracted to it. In early May 1942 Squires was discharged from the Constabulary and he another former policeman, Samuel Drover, went by train to Whitbourne to undergo Ranger training. However, Squires only served six months as a

Ranger and resigned in December 1942. That spring, May to be exact, he married Vera Sellars of Western Bay and they had six children: Malcolm, Ruth, Wilfred, David, Carol Ann and Nancy.

In 1944, Malcolm Squires went to work at Her Majesty's Penitentiary and became Superintendent. He remained there until his retirement in February 1980. From 1983 until his death on June 20, 2004, Squires lived with his youngest daughter in Mount Pearl.

Regimental Number 116 - Samuel Drover

#116

Samuel "Sam" Drover was born in 1911 in Hodge's Cove, Trinity Bay. His father was Captain Samuel Drover, his mother Hannah Pond. Sam Jr. was one of nine children.

Sam was not only a Newfoundland Ranger, but was the MHA for White Bay district from 1949 - 1956, making him one of only two ex-Rangers to be elected representatives (the other being Bill Smith # 56).

Sam was educated at Hodge's Cove and worked as a teacher and served as a member of the Newfoundland Constabulary for four years.

In the spring of 1942 he joined the Newfoundland Rangers after being rejected for the RCAF due to a heart murmur. He was now 31 years old. He was posted to detachments in Meadows, Port aux Basques, Lamaline and La Scie.

While stationed in Port aux Basques, Sam helped recover bodies from the sinking of the SS Caribou in October 1942. He was eventually promoted to Corporal. In1945, he wed Daphne Butler of Port Rexton.

In 1949, Drover was elected to the first House of Assembly after Confederation as the Liberal member for White Bay, his old Ranger territory.

According to the Dictionary of Newfoundland Biography, Drover left the Liberal Party in 1956 and sat as a member of the Cooperative Commonwealth Federation (CCF) Party, the first person to represent that Party in Newfoundland.

Drover was defeated as the CCF candidate in the general election later that year and ran unsuccessfully in several subsequent elections. He returned to teaching and then private business in Hodge's Cove and passed away in June 2005 at the age of 94 years.

#117

Regimental Number 117 - Andrew Chynne

Andrew Chynne was working in the lumber woods with his father when he was fourteen years old. He was a tough, experienced outdoors man by the time he joined the Rangers in June 1942.

He was born in Laurenceton on March 15, 1918, to John and Ellen Chynne. Even though he went to work in the woods at fourteen, he kept a hand in the school books and completed grade eleven at Prince of Wales College.

Andrew joined the Air Force but was discharged due to color blindness. He joined the Rangers in June 1942 and was stationed at Belleoram, Nain, Grand Bank, St. Lawrence, St. George's and Fortune. He served a total of five years and six months.

In 1944, he wed Mazie Williams and they had one son Gary. After leaving the Rangers, Andrew managed the Toronto firm of MacDonald Appliances for 25 years. He retired to the Lewisporte area.

#118

Regimental Number 118 - Ferdinand Davis

Ferdinand "Ferd" Davis was born in Grand Falls in May 1916. His father John was an employee of the A.N.D. Company, while his mother Gertrude (Hatch) was a homemaker.

After completing grade eleven in Grand Falls, young Ferd went to work with the A.N.D. company in their Grand Falls mill.

On June 25, 1942, he joined the Newfoundland Rangers seeking adventure and loving the outdoors. He was posted to detachments at Twillingate, North West River, La Scie and Glenwood.

While stationed in Glenwood he lead a crew to the crash site of a Belgian Sabena aircraft near Dead Wolf Lake. He helped bury 26 dead on site, and rescued the 18 survivors.

In 1943, he married Hazel Jeffries and they had two children; John and Paula. Ferd served for almost 6-1/2 years and was discharged in November 1948 on compassionate grounds, following the death of his wife.

In 1949, he began work as a social worker with the provincial government of Newfoundland, retiring from the public service in 1978.

He died on November 11, 1993 at age 77. He passed away in the 11th hour, of the 11th day of the 11th month.

Regimental Number 119 - John Howard

#119

John Howard was the son of fisherman Joseph Howard and Sarah Jane Milley. He was born on Christmas Day 1919. After completing grade eleven he joined the Ranger Force in June 1942. He served for 7 years and was posted to Makkovik, Hopedale, Hebron, Flower's Cove and Twillingate.

John decided against joining the RCMP in 1949 and he went to work in mining exploration with Gullbridge Mines. He worked in Gull Pond, Little Bay, Baie Verte (as supervisor of Advocate Mines) and then in Sudbury, Ontario, as a geologist. In 1956, he married Monica Dempsey and they had two daughters, Margaret and Terri.

John's daughter Margaret recalls a story her father used to tell about his days as a Ranger. It seems that he had to escort a mentally ill patient to St. John's and while traveling on the train the mentally ill person became very disturbed. In attempt to quiet the sick man, the Ranger began to sing a song. The person quieted down but when the song ended, John Howard asked the person how was the song, to which the patient replied that he would cause no more trouble if only the Ranger promised not to sing anymore. Margaret said whatever attributes her father might have had singing wasn't one of them since he couldn't carry a tune of any kind.

Regimental Number 120 - Earl Brazil

#120

Earl Brazil was born in Battle Harbor, Labrador, June 28, 1922. His father Stanley was a wireless operator, his mother Lavenia a homemaker.

Earl attended school in both Battle Harbor and at Bishop Feild College in St. John's.
Sometime after completing high school he joined the Rangers and was stationed at Northwest River, Goose Bay and Hopedale.

On August 23, 1948, he wed Margaret Harvey and they had three children: Patricia, David and

John. Earl supported his family by working as a wireless operator in Northern Posts, like his father.

#121

Regimental Number 121 - Howard Richards

Howard Richards joined the Rangers in June 1942. He served for five years and was posted to the Quartermaster's Stores, Stephenville, Rose Blanche and Point Leamington.

He was born in Port Union on March 18, 1925, to George and Ettie (Batten) Richards. After completing high school he joined the Ranger Force and remained one until July 1947.

In 1962 he wed Rita Mahoney and they had one son, Howard. The couple lived in Gander where Howard Sr. worked as an air traffic controller. He stayed in this occupation for 32 years.

Many years after he had left the Rangers, Howard received a package in the mail one day. It was his old Ranger Force handcuffs with his name imprinted on them. They were donated for archival purposes.

His brother Roy was Ranger # 174.

#122

Regimental Number 122 - Lewis Noseworthy

Lewis Noseworthy was born November 1912 in Pouch Cove. His father Allen was a fisherman, his mother Margaret a homemaker.

Lewis finished high school in Pouch Cove and then completed one year of university at which time he went to work as a schoolteacher.

He joined the Rangers in June 1942 and was posted to various detachments over the next eight years. He served at Petite Forte, Forteau and Red Bay.

In June 1944, he wed Lexie Barby and they had three children: Paul, Lewis and Marilyn. In 1950, Lewis transferred to the RCMP and served with that Force for 17 years, retiring as a Corporal. From 1968 to 1976, he worked as a security guard at the Fisheries College in St. John's. He eventually settled in Mount Pearl.

Lewis died in October 1993.

Regimental Number 123 - James Bragg

James "Jim" Bragg was a fisherman before he became a Ranger. And, he later went on to be a cop in one of Canada's biggest cities.

#123

He was born in Pouch Cove on December 9, 1920. His father James was a fisherman, while his mother Jessie (Williams) looked after the home and family. He completed grade eleven and went to work in the fishing boat with his father.

Jim joined the Rangers in 1942 and remained in the Force for four years. He was posted to Hopedale, St. George's, Fortune, Grand Bank and Stephenville Crossing. His brother Ambrose was also a Ranger (# 130).

In 1947, he married Leona (Gardner) and they had four children: Jim, Robert, Lynda and Janet.

In 1948, he joined the Metro Toronto Police Department where he served for twenty seven years. After leaving the police force in 1975, he worked with Sears Canada for ten years.

The Braggs settled in Willowdale, Ontario, and Jim passed away on January 22, 2002. His wife recalls that his life-long friend and fellow Ranger Jack Luscombe passed away a couple of months later.

Regimental Number 124 - Earl Rose

Earl Rose was another Ranger who was a policeman through and through. He was a member of the Newfoundland Constabulary prior to joining the Rangers, and he served for over twenty-five years in the RCMP after the Rangers were absorbed by that force.

#124

Rose was born at St. Lawrence on July 11, 1920, to Mary Ellen and Alexander Rose. He was educated at St. Matthews school in St. Lawrence and after high school entered the Newfoundland Constabulary. This makes him one of twenty-two Rangers who transferred from the Constabulary to the Rangers.

Earl stayed with the Constabulary a short time before he entered the Rangers in July 1942. "I entered the Rangers as the work offered more challenges and diversification. I also had a liking for the outport type of life," Earl says.

He remained a Ranger until 1950 and was posted to various

detachments including Stephenville Crossing, Goose Bay, Bay L'Argent, Belleoram, Port aux Basques, Grand Bank, Hermitage; Pushthrough; Burgeo and Glenwood. Rose recalls the great comradeship that came from associating with young men from all over Newfoundland.

The year 1950 was a momentous one for Earl Rose. Not only did he join the RCMP when it swallowed the Rangers, but he was also married to Dorothy Oldford.

Earl retired from the RCMP in 1975 as a Staff Sgt. Major with an honourable discharge and the long service medal. He died in 2005.

Regimental Number 125 - Jim Coffin

#125

Jim Coffin was born in Recontre East on June 27, 1922, the son of Clarence and Emily Coffin. After finishing school in his home town, Jim completed first year university. Prior to entering the Rangers he was a school teacher, and also worked at the U.S. base at Argentia. But in 1942 Jim's life changed forever when he joined the Rangers. A family member recalls that Jim felt that entering the Rangers was "a worthy vocation."

He remained with the Rangers for six years and was posted to Port aux Basques, Rose Blanche and Marystown.

In July 1945, he married Myrtle Cluett and they had three children: Elaine, Clarence and James (deceased).

After leaving the Rangers in 1948, Jim Coffin worked in retail business marketing. But Jim never really got the chance to make his mark in a post-Ranger career as he passed away on July 20, 1956 at the age of 34.

Regimental Number 126 - Matthew Butler

Matthew "Matt" Butler was born in St. John's on March 26, 1924. His father William was a fisherman, his mother Ida (Legrow) operated a grocery store.

Matt was educated in Bauline and after finishing grade eleven (commercial) he worked in the accounting department at Fort Pepperrell.

He joined the Rangers in December, 1942, and served for almost five years. He was posted to Deer Lake, Glenwood, Meadows and Belleoram.

#126

On September 6, 1947, he wed Hilda (Hodder) and they had two sons: William and Garrett. From the early 1950s, Matt worked at the Waterford Hospital in St. John's as a physiotherapy attendant.

Regimental Number 127 - Thomas Fitzpatrick

Thomas "Tom" Fitzpatrick was born in Marystown on October 15, 1923. His father John was a customs officer while his mother Mary (Grant) was a home-maker. He completed grade eleven in Marystown and went to work with a survey crew in St. John's.

He joined the Rangers between December 1942 and late January 1943. He was stationed at Twillingate but did not serve his full five year hitch due to ill health, and he is not found on the November 30, 1945 personnel list regarding discharges.

#127

In 1956, Tom married Dete (Bucey) and they had four children: Donna, Lynn, Joseph and Paula. The couple settled in Marystown and operated a supermarket and wholesale business. Tom's brother Gordon was Ranger # 24.

Regimental Number 128 - Eugene Greene

#128

Eugene Greene was born in Bishop's Falls on November 5, 1923. John, his father, was a bartender, while Elsie (Warren), his mother, tended to the family and home.

He finished grade eleven in Bishop's Falls and went to work as a Constable with the Newfoundland Constabulary. In January 1943 he joined the Rangers. But he left the Rangers in May that year and joined the Newfoundland Artillery. Upon arriving in England he was transferred to the 166th field regiment and served throughout the Italian campaign. After being discharged in 1945, he worked with the Newfoundland forestry department and settled in Botwood.

He married Mary Lidstone in 1947 and they had five children: Wayne, David, Howard, Sandra and Pauline.

Regimental Number 129 - Walter Swyer

#129

Walter Swyer was the son of a fisherman, Francis, who drowned in 1924 while sailing aboard the schooner "Donna Silver." His mother, Irene (Hulan), was a manager of a general store and also a postmistress.

Walter was born May 1922 in Sandy Point. He finished school in Robinson's and later attended Dalhousie University. He joined the Rangers in early 1943 and was promoted to second class Ranger. But he left the Force sometime before the end of 1945.

He never married and settled in Edmonton, Alberta, where he worked as a heavy equipment operator. He later relocated to Cartyville, Newfoundland.

Regimental Number 130 - Arthur Bragg

#130

Arthur "Art" Bragg was another fisherman's son. His father James fished out of Pouch Cove, while his mother Jessie (Williams) tended to the family and home.

Art was born in November 1917 and completed grade eleven in Pouch Cove. After finishing school he worked in the cod trap fishery with his father.

In March 1943, he joined the Newfoundland Rangers but he only served two months and two days due to color blindness.

He married Edith Braun and they had one son, John. The family settled in Kitchener, Ontario where Art worked as a master carpenter. Ranger James Bragg, # 123, was his brother.

Regimental Number 131 - Cyril Lynch

#131

Cyril Lynch was born November 30, 1923, to James Lynch, a linesman, and Gertrude (Reddy). He earned grade eleven commercial at St. Patrick's Hall School in St. John's and then followed in his father's footsteps and went to work as a linesman with Avalon Telephone Company.

The Rangers attracted Cyril because it promised a better job than the one he held and so he enlisted. But he served only about six months when he resigned to go overseas. He joined the Canadian Army Corps of Signals and was awarded volunteer service medal, the defense of England and France medals, and the liberation of Holland medal.

After the war, he married Katherine Mary Hickey and they had six children: William, David, Cyril Jr., Joseph, Anne and Mark.

#132

Regimental Number 132 -Allan Noseworthy

Allan Noseworthy was born on February 23, 1923, in the little fishing community of Pouch Cove. He was the eldest of seven children and the son of a fisherman/farmer.

After completing school, Allan worked as a teacher at Byscane Cove at Cape St. Francis. He was encouraged to join the Rangers by # 130 Ambrose Bragg. He was also attracted to the Force because his uncle, M.L. Noseworthy, was Ranger # 122.

However, after training Allan declined a posting to a Ranger detachment for personal reasons. He recalls the Chief Ranger, R. D. Fraser , was livid. He had to pay for the cost of his training, about $200.

Allan returned to Memorial University College and completed a third year teaching certificate. In 1951, he wed his wife Audrey. They had four children: Lance, Lex, Larry and Lindsay.

Allan had an outstanding business career with Steer's Ltd. managing their western Newfoundland operation, which he later purchased. In 1975-76 he served as president of the Ranger Force Association.

Regimental Number 133 - Angus Campbell

Angus Campbell is another man who served only a short time as a Ranger before moving on to a distinguished career as an architect.

He was born May 25, 1924, in St. John's. His father John was a fish broker and his mother Mary a housewife.

He attended St. Bon's where he excelled in sports and earned grade eleven commercial. He joined the Ranger Force around May 1943 after completing school. However, while posted to Barracks and waiting for his uniform to arrive he decided to seek a career in designing buildings.

He articled with the architectural firm of W.J. Ryan and worked there for about seven years. Then he branched out with George Cummings under the banner "Cummings and Campbell." He distinguished himself in designing buildings like the former home of Premier J.R. Smallwood, Carnell's Funeral Home, St. Pius Tenth Roman Catholic Church, Carbonear Hospital, and Beth El Synagogue, for which he won an award for modern architecture. He settled in St. Phillip's.

Regimental Number 134 - Henry Winsor

#134

Henry "Harry" Winsor was born April 18, 1911. His father Henry was a marine Captain, while his mother Mary (Hurley) looked after the home and family.

Harry was baptized by Rev. Father E.P. Roche on April 21, 1911, at the Basilica of St. John the Baptist. The baptism was witnessed by William Ryall and Anastasia Hurley.

Harry completed grade eleven in St. John's and joined the Royal Newfoundland Artillery (Reg. No. 970-730) where he served overseas from May 1940 to May 1942. It is thought that he was discharged from the artillery to look after family matters when both his parents died within the space of one year.

Harry joined the Ranger Force in mid-1943 and was stationed at the Quartermaster's Stores. He served a total of about fifteen months with the Rangers and later was employed with the Provincial Department of Highways.

Regimental Number 135 - Raymond House

#135

Raymond "Ray" House's father was a postal worker and his mother Mary (Stevenson) was a homemaker. His brother Bob was also a Ranger (# 202).

Ray was educated at Parade St. School and Parkins Academy. Prior to joining the Rangers, Ray worked with a construction company excavating tunnels in the Southside hills in St. John's.

He joined the Rangers in 1942 because of the lure of the rugged outdoor life. He saw postings to detachments in Lewisporte and Stephenville. Ray remained a Ranger until 1945 at which time he left the Force.

He wed Anna Marie Hynes and they had two daughters; Annette, a nurse, and Maureen a teacher.

After leaving the Rangers , Ray worked at Harmon U. S. Air Force Base in Stephenville. Later he ran his own garage and service station in Stephenville. He went on to become parts manager at Corner Brook Garage from where he retired.

Regimental Number 136 - Donald Ford

Donald Ford was not only a Ranger but was also a submariner in the Royal Navy. He was born October 1, 1923, on Fogo Island to Zebedee and Janet (Hodder), who ran a store. He earned grade eleven at Joe Batt's Arm, Fogo Island and was just out of school when he joined the Ranger Force in mid-1943. His brother Jim was also a Ranger (# 138).

He served a brief time before joining the Royal Navy but was invalided out of the war when a torpedo fell out of position on a submarine and injured his hand. After his naval service he worked as a diesel mechanic and settled in Toronto, Ontario.

#136

Regimental Number 137 - Clayton Gilbert

Clayton Gilbert was a big, strong man and Ches Parsons recalls he had a reputation for his strength. Parsons was posted to a detachment recently vacated by Gilbert. A local hard case asked Parsons what he would do if he had to arrest him. Before Parsons could answer, the man's wife intervened and said, "Remember what happened when you challenged Ranger Gilbert. You were crawling around the house for a week. You had better not try your antics on this Ranger as I have no intentions of looking after you again."

#137

Clayton Gilbert was born in Haystack on September 15, 1922. His father, John, was a marine trader, while his mother Julia (Paul) looked after the house.

He completed high school in Haystack and went to work as a policeman with the Newfoundland Constabulary. But in July 1943 he joined the ranks of the Newfoundland Rangers. In seven years as a Ranger he was stationed at Port aux Basques, North West River, Port Saunders and Grand Bank.

While still a Ranger, Clayton married Dinah (Petten). They had two children, Keith and Diane.

Clayton became a Mountie in 1950. He was killed in an auto accident while serving in the RCMP in 1954.

Regimental Number 138 - James Ford

James "Jim" Ford had a near death experience while serving in the Rangers. He was patrolling by dog sled in the Hebron area when the sled went over a steep embankment and Ford was completely buried in snow. He was eventually rescued by the sled driver. Ford's wife recalls that Jim was never as terrified before or after that event.

Jim Ford was born in Joe Batt's Arm, Fogo Island, on November 9, 1919. He was the brother of Donald Ford (# 136), the son of Zebedee and Janet (Hodder). Jim completed high school on

#138

Fogo Island and went to work at the St. John's Dockyard. He joined the Rangers in mid-1943.

In five years of Ranger service he was posted to Hopedale, Hebron and Rose Blanche. He left the Rangers in September, 1948 when his five year hitch expired.

That same year he married Edith Farrell and they had four children: Lloyd, Phyllis, Kenneth and Adrian.

After leaving the Rangers Jim worked as a mechanic, including a stint with the town of Coburg, Ontario. He eventually settled in the Coburg area.

Regimental Number 139 - Earl Hart

Earl Hart put his Ranger training and experience in dealing with people to good use. After retiring from the Rangers he was employed as a social worker by the provincial government and later was a magistrate.

He was born at Champney's East, Trinity Bay, on January 9, 1922 to Joseph and Eliza Hart. Earl completed high school at Champney's East and took some courses at Memorial University College. After finishing high school, he worked with A. Harvey and Company and spent time overseas in Scotland with the Newfoundland Forestry Unit.

#139

Earl joined the Rangers in 1943. "I felt it was a challenge and an opportunity to meet people and see new communities in Newfoundland and Labrador," he says.

He married Janet Nippard in October 1945. They had four children: Daphne, Lorne, Geraldine and Barbara.

As a Ranger, Earl was posted to St. Lawrence, Flowers Cove and Cartwright. He recalls how isolated things were in Labrador at that time. "Myself and my wife opened our Christmas cards on Good Friday," Earl recalls. He has vivid memories of the isolation of the Labrador coast in the 1940s.

While stationed in St. Lawrence on the Burin Peninsula, he remembers many raids for contraband liquor from the French Islands of St. Pierre and Miqueleon. He served his full five year term and left the Rangers in 1948.

After leaving the Rangers, Earl spent over twenty years as a social worker and Magistrate with the Provincial Government.

#140

Regimental Number 140 - Expedite Howard

Expedite Howard joined the Newfoundland Rangers in mid-1943 and served seven years and one month. He left the Rangers in 1950 when the RCMP took over policing outport areas.

Expedite was born in Daniel's Cove on May 26, 1921, to Lawrence and Margaret Howard. He went to school in Daniel's Cove and Grates Cove and earned grade eleven.

After finishing high school, Expedite taught school for one year in Fleur de Lys. But he was so impressed by the local Ranger that the next year he applied to join the Force.

Howard was interviewed by the Stephenville newspaper "The Georgian" on May 21, 2002, and he fondly recalled the 16-1/2 months he was posted to Labrador. "I was treated like a celebrity. People always took me into their homes for a meal," he said.

Ranger Howard was on motorcycle patrol near Stephenville with # 166 Michael Collins when the machine the two were traveling on left the road. In the resulting crash, Collins was killed, but Howard was unscathed.

In 1947, Expedite married Alicia Delaney and they had four children: Linda, Leona, Daniel and Darlene.

Howard joined the RCMP in 1950 and spent fifteen years with that police force before he had enough of policing. He then supported his family by working with the provincial motor vehicle registration division. Expedite Howard is retired and living in Stephenville as this book goes to print.

Regimental Number 141 - Jack Jacobs

Jack Jacobs was born on January 26, 1923, in Harbour Grace. His father was Peter and his mother was Henrietta (Strange). Peter Jacobs was a policeman and perhaps this law enforcement background attracted the young Jack to the Newfoundland Rangers.

#141

Jack finished grade eleven in Harbour Grace and joined the Royal Air Force. Illness forced him out of forces and so in 1944 he joined the Rangers because it was a good job.

He served from 1944 to 1950 and was posted to St. George's, Port Saunders, Harbour Breton, Pushthrough and Springdale.

In September 1945, he married Rita Collins and they had nine children: Helen, Deli, Bob, Judi, Jack, Janet, Glen, Susan and Paul.

After leaving the Rangers in 1950, Jack was manager of A.E. Hickamn Ltd. in Corner Brook.

Regimental Number 142 - Charles Davis

Charles Davis went overseas with the 166 Heavy Artillery where he attained the rank of Sergeant. He was wounded in action in Tunisia, North Africa, and was evacuated in 1943 to return home. He joined the Ranger Force that year and served for a short time before leaving.

#142

Charles was born in Harbour Grace in May 1919. His father Robert was a surveyor and his mother Maude (Cox) looked after the home.

He married Charlotte Elliot in October 1946 and they had five children: Jerome, Shirley, Cathy, Joan, Maureen.

Charles settled in Corner Brook where he worked as a customs collector, a job he held until his death in 1972.

Regimental Number 143 - Martin Barron

Martin Barron was born August 4, 1912, in Placentia. His father John was a fisherman and his mother Anne (Furlong) a domestic worker. He completed high school and earned grade eleven.

He joined the Rangers near the end of 1943 and was posted to the Ranger Force patrol boat at Pushthrough. He served approximately 2-1/2 years and then joined the Newfoundland Customs Preventive Service. About 1958 he began work with the St. John's pilotage service, eventually becoming a skipper on one of the boats.

In July 1970 Martin married Violet Chaytor. The couple had no children.

#144

Regimental Number 144 - James Chancey

James "Jim" Chancey was born in December 1927 in St. John's. He completed high school at Prince of Wales College and joined the Rangers in 1943. He served about two years before leaving the Force.

One thing which influenced him to join the Rangers was the fact his brother Robert (# 69) was in the Ranger Force.

He married Maureen Annonson and they had six children: Bob, Rhonda, Paula Jean, Blaine, Peter and Eric.

Jim eventually settled in Vancouver, British Columbia, and worked as a construction manager in many locations. He retired to his hometown of St. John's and married Isabel. He passed away in June 1996.

Regimental Number 145 - James McCue

You might say that James "Jim" McCue had a "hot and cold" career. He served as a member of both the Newfoundland Constabulary and the Ranger Force before working as a firefighter on the U.S. bases in Argentia and Goose Bay.

Jim was born in Fox Harbour, Placentia Bay, on July 25, 1922. His father James was a Boston and Placentia Bay fisherman, while his mother Cecilia (Cleary) was a housewife.

After finishing grade eleven he worked with the Newfoundland Constabulary for a few months in 1943. Then he joined the Rangers, where he stayed but a few months.

He eventually found his calling as a firefighter at the U.S. bases in Newfoundland, Labrador and Greenland.

Jim married Elizabeth Healey in April 1950 and they had four children: Gerard, Patrick, Brian and Donna.

Regimental Number 146 - Thomas Redmond

Thomas "Tom" Redmond loved the countryside as a young man, so it was a natural thing for him to join the Rangers. Today in retirement Tom still spends most of his time in the country at his cabin in Mahers.

Tom was born in St. John's on October 26, 1922, to Thomas and Isabelle (Holden). His father worked in the office of the railway and his mother looked after the home and family. He completed grade twelve at St. Bon's and completed a course in stenography.

After finishing high school he worked for about a year at the U.S. base in Argentia. Tom recalls how it was he came to be in the Rangers.

"I was working in Argentia and met a man who had been in the Rangers. I was interested in seeing the countryside so I joined the Rangers in February 1944. There were about eight men in my class and we trained in Kilbride under Sgt. Peckford," Tom says.

Tom remembers most of the men in his Ranger class. They included: Charles Davis, Martin Barron, Bill Walsh, Jim McCue, Jim Chancey, Kevin Ryan.

Tom served five years as a Ranger including a stint in Forteau, Labrador. He recalls that most of his work included social work and relief administration. He was later posted to detachments in Cartwright, Lanse au Clair, Port Saunders and Springdale.

After leaving the Rangers he went to work with the Department of Health and Welfare as a social worker. He later transferred to the Department of Health where he stayed until his retirement in 1984.

Regimental Number 147 - William Walsh

William "Bill" Walsh joined the Rangers in 1944 and was posted to detachments in Port Hope Simpson, Bay L'Argent and Marystown. He served a total of six years, until 1950.

Bill was born in St. Brendan's, Bonavista Bay, in November 1922. His father David was a fisherman and his mother Elizabeth (Walsh) looked after the home and family.

He completed grade eleven in St. Brendan's and went to work as a surveyor's assistant. But

#147

the attraction of the Ranger Force and the steady employment it offered enticed him away.

In 1948, he married Marion Lawrence and they had two daughters, Winnifred and Evelyn. After leaving the Rangers in 1950, he did a brief stint in the RCMP before taking his discharge by purchase and launching out into the grocery business.

#148

Regimental Number 148 - Kevin Ryan

Kevin Ryan joined the Rangers in 1944 and he must have been a man with a deep spirituality and a heart for serving others. You see, after he left the Rangers he was ordained a Roman Catholic priest.

He was born in Calvert, Newfoundland, in 1924, one of nine children of Michael and Bridget (Clancy). His father was a post master and his mother a telephone operator. He did his early schooling in Calvert then went to St. Bon's for grades ten, eleven and twelve.

Kevin's sister Marie, herself a Presentation nun, recalls that Kevin was rejected for the Air Force because of his hearing and so he decided to join the Rangers. Marie also remembers her brother "as a very compassionate man."

After joining the Rangers he was posted to detachments in Lamaline and Port au Port. He responded to the wreck of the SS Fernfield with Ranger Jack Fagan. No doubt the rugged outdoor life attracted Kevin because his sister Marie recalls that he enjoyed "trouting and all the outdoor stuff."

But the life of the social worker/policeman was not for him. He felt a divine calling and so he decided to become a Catholic priest.

He studied at St. Peter's Seminary in London, Ontario, and was ordained in 1954. As when he was a Ranger, he moved around the outport areas of the province and served in Stephenville, St. Alban's, Cape St. George, Benoit's Cove, Codroy Valley, Corner Brook and Stephenville Crossing.

Rev. Father M. O'Quinn, parish priest, worked with Father Kevin and described him as a builder and pointed to the beautiful churches he organized in Benoit's Cove and St. Andrew's, Codroy Valley.

But not only was he a priest, Father Kevin was a life-long member of the Knights of Columbus Archbishop Howley Council in Corner Brook.

Kevin's sister-in-law, Hannah Ryan, recalls that Kevin was an avid reader and possessed a great sense of humour. "He was a jolly man,"

Hannah says. Kevin's youngest brother William "Willie" also entered the priesthood, and, as mentioned, his sister Marie entered the Presentation convent. So the family must have had a strong faith. Sister Marie Ryan says that when she and Kevin were growing up, the family said the rosary together each night and went to church regularly. Coincidentally, Father Kevin Ryan passed away in October 1984, not long after the visit of Pope John Paul II to Newfoundland.

Regimental Number 149 - Thomas Warfield

#149

Thomas "Tom" Warfield was born in Wesleyville to Hubert and Jane Warfield. But he eventually settled in sunny Sonoma, California, a long, long way from foggy Newfoundland.

Tom was educated at Bishop Feild College in St. John's and joined the Rangers in 1944. The lure of police work attracted Tom to the Rangers. "Policework was most appealing to me at the time. My step-brother Ed Warfield was in the Constabulary and perhaps this influenced me," Tom says.

He served five years and several months as a Ranger and was posted to detachments in Stephenville Crossing, Port aux Basques, Burgeo, Codroy Valley, Hopedale and Glenwood.

In 1951, he married Roberta Melbourne, and they had two children, Terry and Rochelle. After leaving the Rangers, Tom worked as an insurance adjuster in Canada and the United States.

Regimental Number 150 - Norman Tiller

#150

Norman Tiller was born in Lumsden, Bonavista Bay, on July 27,1926. His father Cecil was an iron worker who worked in the States, while his mother Flora (Smith) was a homemaker.

Norman graduated from Bishop Feild College in St. John's in 1944 and joined the Rangers that year. However, he served but a short time (less than a year) and was stationed at Lewisporte. He did have at least one memorable experience as a Ranger when he was escorting a prisoner from Harmon Field via train and spent three days stuck on the Gaff Topsails in snow drifts.

In 1956, he married Julia (Keeping) and they had three children: Glen,

Sandra and Robin. He supported the family by working in the auto insurance business, eventually forming and running his own company in Calgary, Alberta.

Regimental Number 151 - Gerard Short

Gerard Short was born in Broad Cove, Conception Bay, on January 14, 1926. His parents were James and Winnifred Sharpe. His mother died in childbirth and he was adopted by Samuel and Mary Short of Kingston, Conception Bay. Samuel was a fisherman and Mary was a school teacher.

Gerard attended St. Joseph's School in Kingston and after completing high school taught school himself at Bryant's Cove.

He joined the Rangers in 1944 and later in life told his daughter Mary of the hardships he witnessed as a Ranger.

He married Sadie (Sarah) Crawford in December 1951 and had a large family of ten children: Rose, Paul, Gregory, Mary, Lucille, Gerry, Joseph, Samuel, Charmaine and Randy.

Gerard supported the family by working at various jobs before entering the trucking and school bus businesses. He passed away on September 28,1994.

#152

Regimental Number 152 - Chesley Parsons

Chesley "Ches" Parsons was born in Parsonsville (formerly Freshwater) Bell Island, Conception Bay on February 20, 1924. His father, John, worked as a fisherman, farmer and miner, while his mother, Mary Ann (Harding), was a book-keeper and homemaker.

Ches attended school at Parsonsville, Bell Island, and graduated from St. Stephen's High School. Prior to entering the Rangers, he worked as a carpenter and a plumber's helper, and he also worked on the U.S. base in Pleasantville.

He joined the Rangers in September 1944 and was posted to Lamaline, Hebron and Port Saunders. He also relieved for short periods at Hopedale and Flower's Cove.

Ches says he joined the Rangers on the recommendation of a Constabulary Officer and of the training he says this:

"Did not find the physical training too strenuous nor the class room lectures boring. The camaraderie was excellent throughout and as a squad of seven we got along unusually well together. As a matter of fact I can't recall one incident of resentment or rancor of any kind. Regretfully only

Norman Tiller, Tom Warfield and I survive. Walter Greene and I who were sworn in at the same time became life long friends."

Ches Parsons served five years and eleven months in the Rangers and left only when the Force was disbanded in 1950. By that time, he had been promoted to Corporal.

He joined the RCMP when it absorbed the Rangers and rose to the rank of Staff Sergeant. He retired from that force in 1972 and spent ten years as a senior customs and excise officer with the Department of National Revenue. He retired from this post in May 1982.

While serving in the RCMP, Ches married Doreen Emily Caines in 1951. The couple had two children, Robert and Glenna (deceased).

Over the course of his RCMP career, Ches was awarded a Canadian Police College Diploma, the RCMP long service medal and a certificate in appreciation for his valued contribution in establishing the RCMP in Newfoundland. After retirement from the Customs and Excise office, he was awarded a certificate for more than thirty-seven years service in the Public Service of Canada.

Ches played a lead role in the creation of this book. He was instrumental in uncovering information on deceased members of the Ranger Force.

Regimental Number 153 - Walter Greene

#153

Like Ches Parsons, # 152, Walter Greene started as a Ranger, joined the RCMP, and finished with that force as a Staff Sergeant.

Walter was born in St. John's on March 15, 1921, to Augustus and Magdalena Greene. He attended school in Cape Broyle and finished high school there. He also received some post-secondary education.

He joined the Rangers on September 5, 1944, after being rejected for Air Force service because of his color blindness. He was posted to Goose Bay, Lamaline and Harbour Breton.

In 1947, he married Mary Collins of Lamaline and they had seven children: Walter, Charles, Gary, Karen, Elizabeth, Peter and Gregory.

In 1950, he opted to join the RCMP when it took over Ranger duties. He was stationed in various communities in Newfoundland and retired from this force in 1973 as a Staff Sergeant. At that time, he relocated to Vancouver, B.C. to work as chief of security for Cadillac Fairview Inc. While employed in that position he helped apprehend some bank robbers and was formally recognized by the Vancouver Police Department.

Regimental Number 154 - Raymond Baird

Raymond "Ray" Baird was from Twillingate on the northeast coast. He was born on April 21, 1925. His father Harold was a blacksmith, his mother Louise (nee Luther) a homemaker.

Ray finished high school in Twillingate and joined the Rangers in September 1944. He was with the Rangers until 1947 and saw postings to Deer Lake and Grand Bank.

In 1947, he wed Grace Caravan. They had one daughter Marilyn who now resides in North Bay, Ontario.

#154

After leaving the Rangers, Ray worked with Bowaters Paper Company in Hare Bay, then moved to Toronto where he was employed with the firm of George Crothers in sales.

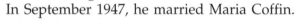

#155

Regimental Number 155 - Clive Strong

Clive Strong was born in Jackson's Cove, Green Bay, on August 1, 1920. His mother Matilda was a teacher and his father Charles a carpenter. Clive finished high school in Jackson's Cove school and worked with his father as carpenter.

He joined the Rangers in September 1944 because he had a real interest in police work. He was posted to Port aux Basques, Burgeo and Cartwright. He served a total of five years and 11 months as a Ranger.

In September 1947, he married Maria Coffin. They had five children: David, Shirley, Robert, Marie and Derek.

Maria remembers the isolation in Cartwright when Clive would be gone on dog sled patrol for three weeks at a time. She also remembers he had a patrol boat that wasn't too reliable.

In 1950, Clive decided to continue policing and joined the RCMP when it absorbed the Rangers. He retired from the Mounties in 1977 and settled in Corner Brook.

Regimental Number 156 - Joseph Lawrence

Joseph Lawrence was born in Channel, Port aux Basques, in 1927. He was named after his father, who worked with the Newfoundland railway. His mother Julia was a homemaker. He completed grade eleven at St. James Anglican school in Channel and worked with the Newfoundland Customs Department before he joined the Rangers in December 1944.

#156

Joseph was posted to Kilbride, Stephenville Crossing, Springdale, St. Lawrence and Fortune. He left the Rangers in May 1947, and married Eva Sulley in St. Anthony in 1949. The couple had two children, Dennis and Orville.

After leaving the Rangers, he supported his family by working as an accountant with Bowaters paper company in Corner Brook. He later became Administrator of the hospital in St. Anthony. Today, he and his wife reside in St. Anthony.

Regimental Number 157 - Randell Haynes

Randell Haynes was born July 20, 1923, in Catalina, Trinity Bay. He was one of eight children born to Lieut. William Haynes, DCM, and Annie (Randell) a school teacher.

He completed grade eleven at St. Peter's Church of England School in Catalina and then worked with Martin Royal Stores on Water Street in St. John's.

Randell joined the Rangers in 1944 and served until 1950, at which time he joined the RCMP as a second class Constable. He served with that force until 1973 when he retired as a Corporal.

#157

As a Ranger he was posted to Battle Harbour and Lamaline. People remember he had a police dog named Prince.

#158

Regimental Number 158 - Cyril Goodyear

Cyril Goodyear is perhaps one of the most well known Rangers. He is the author of several books, the ex-Mayor of Deer Lake, and he also served in the RCMP and as Chief Provincial Court Judge.

Goodyear was born in Deer Lake in 1926. His mother Mary (Hicks) was a homemaker, while his father, Theophilus Goodyear, was a logging contractor. Cyril went to school in Deer Lake and after finishing high school joined the Royal Canadian Air Force. After leaving the RCAF he joined the Rangers in 1945 because, "I was looking for a job and Corporal John Hogan told me about a vacancy."

As a Ranger he was stationed in Kilbride, Battle Harbour, Nain, Port aux Basques, Rose Blanche and Gambo. He married Shirley Ann Serrick in June 1949 and they had two sons, Brian and Jed. Cyril served a total of five years and two weeks and then joined the RCMP when it absorbed the Rangers.

He remained a Mountie until 1965 at which time he became a Provincial Court Judge. He had completed a Law Degree at Dalhousie University in Halifax, N.S. in the preceding years. Cyril eventually became the top judge in the province and went on to serve in government as Deputy Attorney General and Deputy Minister of Northern Affairs. He and his wife settled in Deer Lake in 1992 where Cyril served as Town Mayor.

#159

Regimental Number 159 - Clifton Matthews

Clifton Matthews was born in Badger, the son of a woods foreman. He completed grade eleven in Badger and worked in the lumber woods with his father.

He joined the Rangers in 1945 and was stationed in Kilbride, Englee, Stephenville and Gambo.

In 1950, Clifton switched to the RCMP when it took over the Rangers' policing duties. He served 35 years with the Mounties and retired in 1980 with the rank of Staff Sergeant.

During the years he was in the RCMP, Clifton married Betsy Matthews and they had seven children: Clifton, Paul, Lorraine, Domick, Phillip, Paulen, and Burt.

Regimental Number 160 - Llewllyn Noel

Llewllyn Noel was born in Harbour Grace on September 30, 1925. His father Robert was a fisherman and his mother Mary a homemaker.

He completed high school in Harbour Grace and prior to joining the Rangers in 1945 was a member of both the Newfoundland Constabulary and the Newfoundland Regiment.

As a Ranger, he was stationed at Burgeo, Stephenville and St. George's. Llewllyn told family members the most attractive part of joining the Rangers was the ability to carry on policing in remote, outport areas.

#160

In 1950, he transferred to the RCMP. In 1953, he married Ella Ball, a nurse from Burgeo and they had five children: Barbara, Donna, Katherine, David and Lori. Eventually, Llewllyn left the RCMP to serve in the Newfoundland Penitentiary Service and was there until he retired December 31, 1973. He and his wife settled in Mount Pearl.

Regimental Number 161 - Allen Stevens

Allen Stevens was born September 30, 1926, to James and Lilly Stevens. His father supported the family by working at Ayre and Sons on Water Street in St. John's.

Allen attended Bond Street School and earned grade eleven. He joined the Rangers in 1945. He was posted to Kilbride, Port au Basques, Gambo, Hermitage and St. Anthony.

In July 1948, Allen married Phyllis Melbourne of Channel Port aux Basques and they had one son, James. In 1950, he transferred to the RCMP and served until 1980, retiring as a Staff Sergeant.

#161

Regimental Number 162 - Reginald Legrow

Reginald "Reg" Legrow lives in Calgary, Alberta, a long way from the isolated shores of Labrador that he once patrolled as a young Ranger.

Reg was born in Broad Cove in February, 1921, to Frederick and Alice LeGrow. He completed high school in Broad Cove and spent five years in the army before joining the Rangers in 1945. Reg says he joined the Rangers because he was looking for a job. "The training was similar to the Army," he recalls.

As a Ranger he was posted to Stephenville Crossing, Port aux Basques, Rose Blanche, LaScie, Port Hope Simpson and Battle Harbour. He has vivid memories of dog sled travel in Labrador

Reg joined the RCMP in 1950 and had a thirty year career as a Mountie. He retired as a Staff Sergeant.

In 1951, he married Gwen, a Welsh nurse, and they had one son, John.

#163

Regimental Number 163 - Edward Lawlor

Edward "Ed" Lawlor had policing in his heart. After a stint as a Ranger he eventually joined the Toronto Police Force.

Ed Lawlor was born in Cappahayden on August 16, 1927. His parents were John and Stella (Tobin) Lawlor. Ed was educated at school in Cappahayden and at St. Bon's College. He joined the Ranger Force in 1945.

He remained a Ranger for two years and was stationed in St. George's and Stephenville. In 1947, he purchased his way out of the Rangers and later that same year he wed Barbara (Cormier). The couple had four children: Wayne, Patricia, Ledon and Gerard.

Ed made his way to Ontario where he worked in the Don Jail for a few years before joining the Toronto Metro Police Department. He settled in Scarborough, Ontario.

Regimental Number 164 - Clarence Brown

Clarence Brown served five years as a Newfoundland Ranger. But he almost died before joining the Rangers when, as a member of the Newfoundland Regiment, he barely escaped from the ill-fated Knights of Columbus Hostel fire in St. John's in December 1942.

Clarence was born at Burnside on March 7, 1912, to William and Mary Brown. After earning grade eleven at Burnside school he taught for a year or two before joining the Newfoundland Regiment.

#164

He joined the Rangers in 1945 and served five years being stationed at Grand Bank and North West River. In 1956, he married Della Butt and they had one son, Richard. The couple settled in Goose Bay where Clarence worked with the Royal Canadian Air Force, the postal department and latterly with the school board.

Regimental Number 165 - Fred Wells

Fred Wells served about two years as a Ranger, but he made his mark in the production and marketing of eggs in this province. He was even inducted into the Agricultural Hall of Fame.

Fred was born at Little Bay, Notre Dame Bay, in March 1927 to Thomas and Mae (Penney). He finished grade eleven in Little Bay and joined the Rangers. As a Ranger he was posted to Bonne Bay.

In May 1949, he married Jane Shears and they settled in Robinson's, Bay St. George. The couple had three sons: Glenn, Paul and John. Fred

#165

supported his family primarily through working as an egg producer. He served for a period as the chairman of the Newfoundland egg marketing board. He was also on the board of directors of the Canadian Egg Marketing Agency.

#166

Regimental Number 166 - Michael Collins

Michael Collins has the sad distinction of being the third member of the Newfoundland Ranger Force to be killed while on duty, the others being Danny Corcoran (# 14) and Michael Greene (# 49).

Michael Collins died while patrolling by motorcycle along the west coast of Newfoundland.

He was born in Lamaline on September 26, 1917, to George and Mary Collins. After finishing high school he enlisted in the Royal Navy. He served on two different ships that were torpedoed. He was invalided out of the Navy.

Collins joined the Rangers in February 1946 and died just six months later. During his short time as a Ranger, he was stationed on board the patrol boat number 303. It seems that Collins, Quarter Master Sgt. Ed Delaney and Chief Ranger Martin were conducting inspections along the south and west coasts of the island. The intention was to leave the boat in La Scie. While en route from Ramea to Burgeo the engine exploded due to gas fumes in the engine room. Thankfully no one was killed, but the boat was disabled. However, by luck the coastal boat S.S. Baccilieu happened along and lent assistance to the Rangers, taking them on board. Following that incident, Collins spent some time in hospital recovering from burns.

Unfortunately, Michael Collins was not so lucky the next time he was involved in an accident. Collins and Ranger Expedite Howard were traveling by motorcycle on patrol between Stephenville and Stephenville Crossing. Howard was riding in the side-car. Whatever happened, the bike went off the road and Michael died as a result of his injuries. He was only twenty-nine at the time of the accident. Ranger Howard escaped unscathed from the tragedy.

Ches Parsons, Ranger # 152, himself patrolled by motorcycle and recalls how off-balance the side-cars made the three-wheeled bikes if the steering was moved too sharply to the right or left. And, of course, in the 1940s, no one wore protective gear such as helmets.

Regimental Number 167 - Reuben Noel

Reuben was born January 25, 1920, in Freshwater, Carbonear, to William and Sara (Moores) Noel. He completed grade eleven in Freshwater, then spent 1936-37 at Memorial University College. He joined the Royal Navy in 1939 and spent the entire war in that service. Upon being discharged in 1946, he joined the Ranger Force and was posted to Grand Bank, Point Leamington, and Deer Lake.

#167

Reuben remained a Ranger until 1950 at which time he joined the RCMP. That same year he married Henrietta Andrews and they had a large family: Barbara, Gary, Rodney, Peggy, Ricky, Deborah, and Gerald.

Reuben Noel only served five years in the RCMP before leaving to work with the Americans at a base in Greenland. Eventually, he worked with the Federal Department of Veteran's Affairs until his retirement in 1980. He spent much of his retirement years at summer homes in Freshwater and Point Leamington. He passed away in 2002.

Regimental Number 168 - Eli John Courage

"Jack" Courage was born in Port Blandford on January 10, 1922. His father Roland ran a store while his mother Grace (Rowe) was a housewife.

After finishing high school he joined the Royal Canadian Air Force (RCAF) where he was a Flight Sergeant. He joined the Rangers in March 1946 and was stationed at Deer Lake. He was discharged on medical grounds in December 1947.

#168

That same year, he wed Audrey Wellon and they had three children: Maureen, Jack and Christine.

He later worked in Administration with the Federal Department of Transport for 34 years. After retirement, he settled in Moncton, New Brunswick.

Regimental Number 169 - Wilbert Wiseman

#169

Wilbert Wiseman was the son of Mary (James) and Pleaman Wiseman of Little Bay Islands. He finished high school and worked in a Bowater's logging camp before he joined the Rangers in March 1946 at age 26.

He served for five years, being posted to Hopedale, Stephenville, Harbour Breton and Belleoram.

In 1950, he joined the RCMP when it absorbed the Ranger force. He wed Kathleen Raymond and they had three children: Sandra, Elizabeth and Barbara.

He died June 26, 1960, while still serving in the RCMP.

Regimental Number 170 - Robert Forward

#170

Robert Forward was born in Little Bay Islands. His parents were James and Hettie, a schooner captain and seamstress respectively.

He finished grade eleven and fished for a time before joining the Rangers in March 1946. He remained a Ranger until the Force disbanded in 1950, and was posted to Port aux Basques, Belleoram, Marystown and Battle Harbour.

Robert says he joined the Rangers as he believed it was a good career path. He joined the RCMP in 1950 when it absorbed the Rangers.

In 1951, he married Emma Hollett and they had four children: Kevin, Donald, Margo and Robert.

Robert left the RCMP in 1966 to join the provincial government's civil service where he worked until retirement.

Regimental Number 171 - Thomas Ford

To say Thomas "Tom" Ford had a varied career is an understatement. Ford served as a Sergeant in the Canadian Army during WW II, then spent time in the Rangers before joining the Mounted Division of the Halifax City Police Department.

Tom was born in Port aux Basques on June 8, 1924, the son of railway agent Joseph Ford and Estelle Shears. After finishing high school he joined the Army. At the end of WWII, he joined the Rangers in 1946. He was instrumental in starting the Royal Canadian Legion Branch 533 in Stephenville and was its first president. He left

#171

the Rangers the following year and married Clara Marriot. They had two children: Mitchell and Marlene. They settled in New Minas, Nova Scotia.

Regimental Number 172 - Abraham Granter

Abraham Granter was born March 10, 1923, in Brookfield. His father Samuel was a fisherman and his mother Ester (Sturge) a housewife. After completing grade eleven he worked with his father in the cod fishery before joining the Rangers in mid-September 1946. But before he completed his training he decided to leave the Rangers, which he did in early October.

He enlisted in the Canadian Army but his length of service could not be determined. He eventually joined the crew of the federal Department of Fisheries vessel, the Hudson, and

#172

was still part of its crew when he died aboard ship in 1973.

Regimental Number 173 - William Mullally

#173

William "Bill" Mullally was born September 12, 1926, in Northern Bay to Lawrence and Mary, a fisherman and housewife respectively.

After finishing high school, Bill completed teacher's training and worked as a school teacher. He joined the Rangers in September 1946 and was posted to Gambo, Port au Port, Goose Bay, Hebron, Hopedale and North West River.

Bill joined the RCMP when it absorbed the Rangers in 1950. In 1952, he wed Genevieve Simms and they had six children: Desmond, Patricia, Carol, David, Yvonne and Robert.

He remained a Mountie until his retirement as a Staff Sergeant in 1981. He earned the Queen's Medal and the Long Service Medal.

Regimental Number 174 - Roy Richards

#174

Roy Richards drove a motorcycle with a side-car while he was in the Rangers. And, he later rose to the rank of Superintendent in the RCMP.

He was born in Port Union on April 3, 1917. His father George kept a store while his mother Ettie (Batten) looked after the home.

Roy joined the Rangers on October 21, 1946, and was posted to St. George's, Port au Port and Stephenville. He remained a Ranger until 1950 at which time he entered the RCMP Following his retirement from the RCMP, he served with the National Parole Board for five years and then with the Moncton Police as Deputy Chief.

He wed Trudy (Kean), his best friend, and they had two children: Lori and Geoffrey. In full retirement he was very active and was involved in a dance group, the Ranger Force Association, and the United Church. He passed away January 5, 2000.

Regimental Number 175 - William Anderson

William "Bill" Anderson was born in British Harbour on December 1, 1924. His father Edmund was a postmaster, and also ran a small general store. His mother Maude (Brown) was a housewife.

#175

After Bill completed grade eleven in British Harbour he worked as a schoolteacher. He joined the Rangers in November 1946 but left for medical reasons while still in training.

On October 20, 1948, he married Frances (Rendell) and they had three children: Corbett, Marilyn and Christopher. Bill supported the family by working with the Post Office and was latterly Postmaster at the Water Street West Post Office. He settled in Mount Pearl.

Regimental Number 176 - Richard Jarvis

Richard "Dick" Jarvis was born in Little Bay West, Fortune Bay, on July 17, 1921. His father Albert was a fisherman who passed away when Dick was only eighteen months old. His mother Frances (Harding) then took Dick and his brother Stephen to live in Belloram.

#176

Dick attended school in Belloram completing grade eleven there. His daughter, Bonnie Jarvis-Lowe, says in the summer of 1939 her father traveled to Harbour Breton for a medical appointment and while there signed up to serve in the British Navy. He was not quite 18 at the time and his mother knew nothing of his joining until he began preparing to leave. By November, he was headed into wartime waters aboard the HMS Shoreham, a Royal Navy sloop. He served in the Mediterranean, Suez Canal, Persian Gulf, Indian Ocean, and all over the Atlantic up until 1942 when he was taken prisoner in North Africa. After a difficult period of captivity, he and his fellow prisoners escaped and spent the next eighteen months running by night and hiding by day. During this time he was reported as missing.

He returned home to his thankful mother at the end of the war in 1945 and joined the Rangers on March 24, 1947. He was posted to Port Aux Basques, Lanse au Clair, Port Hope Simpson and Twillingate.

In April 1948, he married Ethel Trimm of English Point, Forteau Bay, Labrador and they had five children: Yvonne (Bonnie), Margaret, David,

Barbara and Laura (Kathy). All four daughters are nurses, while son David is an electrical technologist with Newfoundland Hydro.

He was honorably discharged from the Rangers and joined the RCMP in 1950 when it absorbed the Ranger Force. He spent 35 years in the RCMP, retiring as a Sergeant. Today, Dick Jarvis lives in Mount Pearl where he is enjoying his retirement.

Regimental Number 177 - Richard Noel

#177

Richard Noel was born in Woody Point, Bonne Bay, to George and Annie Noel, a cook and homemaker respectively. He finished grade eleven in Woody Point and joined the Rangers in March 1947 because it offered a good job. He was posted to Nain, St. George's and Stephenville.

He remembers one incident involving a mentally ill person at Nain which created a lot of work for him. In May 1950, a man was brought to Nain suffering from mental illness but because the coast was ice-bound he had to be kept by Ranger Noel in the Ranger detachment. At night the patient would be placed in a straight jacket on the only bed and the Ranger would sleep on the floor across the doorway. The Ranger also had to cook for the man. This kept up for three months until navigation opened in July. The man was then transported on the S.S. Kyle to St. John's.

Richard subsequently joined the RCMP. He served for thirty years, retiring to pension.

In August 1952 he wed Violet Noseworthy and they had two children: Marjorie and Paul. In 1998, he married for a second time, taking the hand of Jean Day.

Regimental Number 178 - Ernest Flight

Ernest was born in Pouch Cove to Ernest and Elsie Flight. Ernest senior supported the family by fishing and farming. Ernest Jr. went to school at the United Church School in Pouch Cove and earned grade eleven.

He joined the Rangers in May 1947 because he was looking for adventure.

Flight remembers the main attraction at the Ranger training site in Kilbride was the presence of lots of pretty nurses at the Nurses' residence at the nearby Sanatorium.

#178

As a Ranger, he was posted to Stephenville Crossing, Deer Lake, Norris Arm, Englee and Springdale. He served three years as a Ranger and in 1950 opted to join the Canadian Armed Forces instead of going into the RCMP.

Ernest spent 25 years as a Naval Aviation Technician and after retirement settled in Winnipeg, Manitoba. He later inherited and ran his father-in-law's garden center business for 12 years. He still lives in Winnipeg as this book is going to press.

Regimental Number 179 - Harold Roy Batten

Harold Batten was born in 1928 in Twillingate. His father Ken ran a poultry farm and his mother Olive (Evans) looked after the home. He earned grade eleven in Twillingate and then helped his father on the farm from 1945-47.

He joined the Rangers in May 7, 1947, and left August 31, 1947. He returned to work on the family farm. He married Elsa Keefe in 1952 and they had three sons: Garrett, Darrell and Kevin. Harold later joined the Royal Canadian Air Force and held the rank of Flying Officer. He became a navigational instructor at the Air Navigational

#179

School in Winnipeg, Manitoba, and served for twelve years. As well, he served for twelve years as chairman of the Boy Scouts Group Committee in Edmonton, Alberta, where his family was chosen as Family of the Year in 1977. He was also manager of three business enterprises and is a recreational, fishing and camping enthusiast.

#180

Regimental Number 180 - Graham Parrott

Graham Parrott was born in Winterton, Trinity Bay in February 1925. His mother Gladys (Downey) was a homemaker, while his father Clarence was a fisherman, and later worked on the U.S. Base at Argentia. Graham earned grade eleven in St. Luke's Anglican School in Winterton and joined the Rangers in May 1947. He says he joined because of the challenge it offered and the permanent employment it promised. He was posted to Twillingate and Petite Forte.

While traveling from Toslow to Petite Forte in Patrol Boat 304, Parrott and mate Patrick Hayden almost drowned when the make and break engine quit in a storm. The boat drifted and rolled uncontrollably, but the men managed to make it by rowing to Little Bona. The next day, a fisherman repaired the engine and Ranger Parrott paid him out of the monthly contingency fund.

Graham joined the RCMP in 1950. He wed Eva Young in 1951 and they had one child, David. They settled in Toronto, Ontario, after Graham left the RCMP. He later worked with the Scarborough Board of Education.

#181

Regimental Number 181 - Fred Moores

Fred Moores was born in Northern Bay on September 9, 1926, the son of Herb Moores, a carpenter, and Carrie Moores, a homemaker. Fred completed high school in Northern Bay and then did five years of training as a finish carpenter.

He joined the Rangers in 1947 and was posted to Kilbride and Stephenville. When the RCMP absorbed the Rangers, Fred decided to join the Royal Canadian Navy.

He wed Teresa Dollard in 1953 <u>and</u> they settled in Ottawa where they had one son, David.

Regimental Number 182 - Jack Hewitt

Jack Hewitt was born in Joe Batts Arm on September 28, 1919. John, his father, was a fisherman. His mother Lavenia was a homemaker.

After finishing high school in Joe Batts Arm, Jack entered the Royal Navy and served for six years. In June 1947, he joined the Rangers, but took a discharge from the Force a few months later.

In December 1947, he wed Emily (Hancock) and they had six children: Sandra, Wayne, Gail, Carol, Derek and Catherine. Jack supported the family by working with the Newfoundland Custom's Service in Gander. He retired in 1980.

#182

Regimental Number 183 - Reginald Bowering

Reginald "Reg" Bowering was born in Bay Roberts on November 8, 1927. He was the son of Edgar and Helen (Belbin). Edgar ran a sawmill and a general store.

Reg was educated at United Church High School in Coley's Point and did a grade eleven commercial course in 1947. That same year he joined the Rangers and saw postings to Grand Bank, Hebron and Hopedale. Reg was interested in both police work and field work offered by the Rangers. His daughter Elizabeth remembers her father speaking about an outbreak of diphtheria while stationed in Nain when a large number of people died.

#183

He remained a Ranger until 1950 at which time he entered the RCMP. He left the RCMP in 1952 and later that same year he married Olivera Burke. They had one daughter.

After leaving the Mounties, Reg worked in the family business before joining the provincial government as a social worker, something for which his Ranger training and experience had well prepared him. He stayed with the Department of Social Services for the remainder of his working career.

#184

Regimental Number 184 - Frank Cheeseman

Frank Cheeseman was a Ranger for three years and continued his law enforcement career with the RCMP when it absorbed the Ranger Force. He remained a Mountie for thirty years and attained the rank of Staff Sergeant.

Frank was born in Kelligrews on July 8, 1927, the son of electrician Thomas Cheeseman and his wife Maude. He completed grade eleven in Kelligrews. He joined the Rangers in August 1947 in order to obtain full time employment.

In 1953, he wed Joan Bridges and they had two children: Frank and Wendy. For his long years of RCMP service Frank was awarded the Long Service Medal with gold clasp and stars, and the Queen's Jubilee Medal. He lives in St. John's.

#185

Regimental Number 185 - Wallace Bowering

Wallace was born in Coley's Point on January 3, 1926, to Florence and Arthur Bowering. He earned grade eleven at Coley's Point School and went to work with the Newfoundland Railway in St. John's in their freight office.

He joined the Rangers in September 1947 for a "career in police work" and saw postings to Kilbride, Twillingate, Hopedale and Hebron. When the RCMP took over the Rangers in 1950, Wallace joined that organization and served until 1972 when he retired. He then worked with security police at McMaster University in Hamilton, Ontario, for six years before retiring again.

An interesting coincidence happened in Bowering's career. As a Ranger and an RCMP officer, he was posted to Hebron in Labrador. As it turns out, he was the last Ranger posted to that northern community and was also the last Mountie to serve in that town.

During his time in the RCMP, he wed Ruby Hawkins and they had three children: Wallace Jr., Jeanette and Valerie (deceased). Wallace resides in Trenton, Nova Scotia today.

Regimental Number 186 - Elmo Porter

Elmo Porter was born June 7, 1929, in Burin. His father William was a Salvation Army Major and his mother Susan was also a Salvation Army officer. Elmo finished grade eleven at Burin and worked as a school teacher before he joined the Rangers in September 1947. He served for almost two years before leaving.

Following release from the Ranger Force, he joined the Canadian Navy and served as an aircraft mechanic on the aircraft carrier Bonaventure. He served five years and later worked with the Iron Ore Company of Canada in Labrador. He had two sons; Kirk and Grant.

He died at the Palliative Care Unit, Western Memorial Hospital, Corner Brook, on Wednesday September 14, 2005.

Regimental Number 187 - Eric Adams

Eric Adams trained to be Ranger but before taking a posting he resigned to join the United States Air Force. He flew in bomber aircraft and earned the rank of Staff Sergeant.

#187

Eric was born in St. John's on September 6, 1928, the son of James and Mary Adams. James operated a taxi and service station. "I joined the Rangers because I was interested in a military type of work. I found the Ranger training excellent and it served me well in my Air Force career," Eric says. After spending about four years in the Air Force he retired to run a service station like his dad.

Eric wed Marjorie Randell in 1957. He resides in St. John's today.

Regimental Number 188 - George Norman

George Norman retired as the fire chief at Stephenville airport with the Department of Transport. No doubt his time as a Ranger stood him in good stead as fire chief.

He was born February 22, 1929, in Jackson's Arm to Eva Carter and Walter Norman. George earned grade eleven at Jackson's Arm and joined the Rangers in late 1947. In 1949, he married Hilda Russell and they had one son Eric who drowned at age 14.

George was posted to Stephenville Crossing and after the Rangers were dissolved he chose not to go to the RCMP, but instead took work as a firefighter at the U.S. base at Harmon Field, Stephenville. After that he moved to the Department of Transport at Stephenville airport and eventually worked his way up to chief. He passed away on November 26, 2003.

#189

Regimental Number 189 - Jack Murdoch

Jack was born in St. John's on June 8, 1927, the son of William Murdoch and Alice Hunt. He earned grade eleven at Bishop Feild College and joined the Rangers in 1947 for adventure. He was posted to Deer Lake where he saw lots of excitement, especially on Saturday nights when the loggers would often fight. He served about a year and then left the Force.

He wed Lillian Caines and they had five children: Alec, Diane, Heather, Bill and Allison. He settled in Deer Lake and worked as an accountant with Goodyear Humber stores. In 1977, he bought the business and operated it as Murdoch's home hardware. He was active in the Lion's Club, the Canadian Cancer Society and the United Church. He was ordained a United Church clergyman.

#190

Regimental Number 190 - Raymond Pittman

Raymond Pitman was born in Marystown on August 27, 1928. His father was a fisherman and his mother Ida (Farwell) was a homemaker. Raymond completed grade eleven in Marystown and was a carpenter by trade.

He joined the Rangers in April 1948 and served until the Rangers were absorbed by the RCMP. Raymond was posted to Twillingate and Port Saunders.

In 1951, he wed Monica Power and they had a large family: Hilena, Kevin, Raymond, Alvin, Janet, Brian and Paul. He supported his family by working as a carpenter and later as a steel foreman at Marystown Shipyard. Illness eventually compelled him to leave the workforce. He died in 1981.

Regimental Number 191 - Ronald Haynes

Ronald Haynes was born in Catalina on July 7, 1929. He joined the Rangers in May 1948 and served for two years until the RCMP absorbed the Force. He then joined the RCMP and served successfully for many years until tragedy befell him. While still serving as an RCMP senior NCO, he was killed in a car-train accident in Tide Head, New Brunswick, on September 9, 1972.

He is survived by his wife, Florence (Perrett), and five daughters: Judy, Susan, Lorie, Heather and Rhonda.

Regimental Number 192 - Jackson Russell

Jackson was born in Carmanville to the captain of a coastal boat and his schoolteacher wife. He earned grade eleven in Carmanville and joined the Rangers in 1948 because he wanted to be a policeman.

He left police work in 1950 when the RCMP took over the Rangers duties and he went to work with the Iron Ore Company in Labrador. In 1953, he wed Marie Jenkins of Springdale and they had two sons: Larry and Keith. Jackson eventually went to work as a maintenance supervisor with the Green Bay Integrated School Board. Today he resides in Springdale.

#192

Regimental Number 193 - William Inder

William Inder was born in Springdale in July 1929. His parents were Rowena (Clarke) and Bertram, co-owners of a transportation company. William joined the Rangers in spring 1948 after finishing high school in Springdale. However, he left the Rangers before he completed training. He wed Pauline Inder in December 1955 and they had two children: Hans and Gregory.

He was employed in his father's transportation company as a taxi driver and ambulance operator. He was also a member of the Springdale fire department and given the title of Honorary Firefighter.

#193

#194

Regimental Number 194 - Ray Huxter

Ray Huxter was born at Springdale on June 21, 1930. His father Samuel was a logger and game warden at Indian Falls, while his mother Sarah (Hiscock) was a teacher.

Ray joined the Rangers on July 2, 1948, two days after he finished grade eleven. He remained a Ranger until 1950 and then joined the RCMP. However, he did not like the RCMP lifestyle and opted out of that Force in 1951. He worked at various jobs until 1968 at which time he landed employment with three golf courses in the Toronto area. He remained employed at the golf courses until he retired in 1995.

#195

Regimental Number 195 - Anthony Downey

Anthony Downey joined the Rangers in August 1948 to have a career helping others and not be confined to an office all day. He remained with the Rangers until they were taken over by the RCMP. He saw postings to Port Saunders, Deer Lake and Stephenville Crossing.

He was born 1926 in the Codroy Valley and prior to entering the Rangers taught school. In fact, he received teacher's training at Memorial University College.

In August 1951, he married Barbara Randell and they had seven children: Maureen, Bernard, Patricia, Paula, James, Elizabeth and Robert. He settled in Corner Brook and was later Deputy High Sheriff for the west coast and Northern Peninsula.

Regimental Number 196 - Howard Guy

Howard Guy was born at Musgrave Harbour on December 25, 1927. His father, Fred Guy, was a carpenter and his mother, Irene Russell, was a postmistress. He completed grade eleven in Musgrave Harbour and joined the Rangers in July 1948. On June 21, 1949, he married Violet Gillingham and they had two sons: Morley and Wilson. After leaving the Rangers in 1950, Howard fished for a while, then worked as time keeper with Goodyear and Sons. Later he operated a grocery store in Musgrave Harbour.

#196

Regimental Number 197 - Keith Hall

Keith Hall had a long varied law enforcement career that started with the Newfoundland Rangers. Keith was born in August 1930, to Stephen Hall and Mabel Cox. He attended school in St. John's. After completing grade eleven he went to work as a meteorological assistant with the Canadian Department of Transport.

Keith joined the Rangers in August 1948 and saw postings to Stephenville, Stephenville Crossing and Springdale. He joined the Rangers because he was attracted to police work. He recalls a time when the Stephenville post office

#197

was robbed on the first night he was stationed there. He also remembers a jurisdictional dispute with American authorities at Harmon Air Force Base in Stephenville which resulted in his being barred from the base.

In 1950, he joined the RCMP when it absorbed the Rangers. In 1954, he wed Joan Marie Hunter and they had three children: Marilyn, Heather and David.

Keith served with the RCMP until he retired in 1973 as a Sgt. Major. Then he was superintendent of corrections in Halifax until 1979, following which he worked with the Department of Victim's Compensation in Nova Scotia until 1992 when he finally retired.

Regimental Number 198 - Ellwood Reid

Ellwood Reid was born in Green's Harbour on August 19, 1922. His father George was a fisherman and merchant mariner, while his mother Violet (George) was a homemaker.

Ellwood finished grade eleven in Green's Harbour, then completed teacher training at Memorial University College in St. John's. He worked as a schoolteacher prior to joining the Rangers.

In late1948 he joined the Rangers, but research was unable to determine where he was posted, or for how long. It is known he wed Hattie (Plank) and they had five children: Doreen, Elaine, Theodore, Sylvia and Thelma. He later worked as a teacher and a heavy equipment operator. He died tragically in Twin Falls, Labrador, in June 1967.

#199

Regimental Number 199 - Thomas Jenkins

Thomas "Tom" Jenkins was born in Bonne Bay on March 23, 1927. Tom completed school there and then worked with his father. Tom joined the Rangers in October 1948 following in the steps of his brother, Gilbert, Ranger # 67. He served almost two full years and left the Force when the RCMP absorbed the Rangers. He served in the RCMP, but his length of service and date of discharge are not known. Tom then worked with CNT until his retirement in 1965

Regimental Number 200 - G. Tetford

G. Tetford was a Ranger for only one day. He was appointed on October 28, 1948, and discharged on October 29, 1948, for reasons unknown. Because his Christian name could not be ascertained, it was impossible finding out other biographical information.

Regimental Number 201 - Stephen Glavine

#201

Stephen Glavine was born in Bishop's Falls on September 21, 1924. His father Pearce worked in the Abitibi Paper Mill in Grand Falls and his mother Mary (Walsh) was a schoolteacher. He finished grade eleven in Bishop's Falls and joined the Rangers in late 1948. We were unable to ascertain the length of his Ranger service.

He wed Margaret Wells and they had a large family: Mary, Beverly, Sandra, Donna, Stephen, Vincent and Catherine. He supported the family by working with Simpson Sears in Halifax for eighteen years, then as purchasing agent in the maintenance department at St. Clare's Mercy Hospital until his retirement at age 65.

Regimental Number 202 - Robert House

Robert House was born November 6, 1928, in St. John's. His father Frank was a postal worker and his mother Mary (Stevenson) was a homemaker. Robert earned grade eleven at Prince of Wales College and worked as a clerk for Acadia Gas Engines on Water Street.

He joined the Rangers in February 1949 and trained in Kilbride after which he was posted to Port aux Basques. Robert investigated a barn fire in Tompkins on the west coast and the elderly owner of the barn told him his life savings were buried under the building. House spent a half a day digging in the ashes and sure enough located thousands of dollars in cash. Robert served up until the Rangers were absorbed by the Mounties. He elected not to go into the RCMP but went to work with Canada Post.

In 1951, he wed Faith Reader and they had three daughters: Roberta, Peggy and Judy. The family settled in Brookfield, Bonavista Bay, and lived there until recently when heart problems dictated he relocate to St. John's.

#203

Regimental Number 203 - Josiah Butt

Josiah Butt was born in Freshwater, Carbonear, in April 1930. His father Josiah was a fisherman and his mother Mary a housewife. Josiah Jr. completed grade eleven in Freshwater then went directly into the Ranger Force. He served up until the time the RCMP absorbed the Rangers and then as a Mountie for a short period. He then worked with Canadian National Telegraphs for a number of yeas until retirement.

In September 1957, he wed Mary Evely from Flatrock, Carbonear, and they had two sons: Robert and Jeffrey.

Josiah passed away on March 16, 2004, at the palliative care unit of the L.A. Miller Center in St. John's.

#204

Regimental Number 204 - Louis Stuckless

Louis "Lou" Stuckless was the last man to join the Newfoundland Rangers and the last of the Rangers to take their discharge from the RCMP. He signed on with the Rangers in July 1949 and served for one year and eleven days until it was absorbed by the RCMP. He then joined the RCMP and served with that Force for thirty years, retiring as a Staff Sergeant.

Lou was born in Tizzard's Harbour in March 1925. His father Alec was a logger, his mother Alfreda (Jenkins) a homemaker.

Lou was educated at Tizzard's Harbour and at Memorial University College and was a school teacher prior to joining the Rangers.

He wed Sarah Rose in 1954 and they had two girls; Wanda and Sarah He settled in Grand Falls and was later employed by the Federal Government as Returning Officer for Grand Falls-White Bay.

Newfoundland Rangers on parade

1942 Contingent at Whitbourne

Headquarters at Whitbourne built in 1936.

Hebron Ranger station

Last Ranger Force Depot, Killbride - St. John's, 1943 - 1950

Red Bay Detachment, 1946

Glenwood Detachment

Newfoundland Rangers taking a break

#160 Llewellyn Noel

Ranger and Mrs. Morris
Christian at Nain, Labrador

#120 Earl Brazil, Hopedale 1941

#16 E. Delaney, #34 W. Rockwood, #53 J. Suley at Battle Harbour, Labrador

Time for a mug up.

#28 I. Glendinning, #32 J. Carnell, Magistrate H.W. Quinton

#30 Howard Manstan in Ranger uniform at West Port White Bay

#88 G.Percy, left,# 89 T.Kean

#168 Eli John Roland Courage

First group of 30 Rangers with Chief Ranger Leonard Stick.

There were three patrol boats like this. The 301, 302 and 303
were assigned as floating detachments.

#161 Al Stevens, #171Tom Ford, #170 Bob Forward

Ranger Force motorcycle 1949 - 1950

#61 E. Strickland

#118 Ranger F. A. Davis, front,
#123 Ranger Bragg, rear, taken at
Whitbourne 1942-44

#88 Ranger G. Percy

#37 Nelson Forward

#79 John Hogan in uniform after his near death adventure in bush.
With him on stretcher is Corporal Eric Butt.

#189 Jack Murdoch, wedding day

#46 Mathew Davis

#190 Raymond Pittman

#156 J. Lawrence

#164 Clarence Brown, 2nd from left, with some Ranger pals

L-R Inspector R. D. Fraser, chief Ranger 1939 - 44
Major L. T. Stick, chief Ranger 1935 - 1936
Major F. Anderton (RCMP) Training Officer 1st. Class
of Rangers and Chief Ranger 1936 - 39

#194 Ray Huxter, #201 S. J. Glavine

TALES FROM THE FIELD

There were 204 men accepted and certified as Newfoundland Rangers. Each of those who completed the necessary three to four months of training would have had their own story to tell while performing their duties but unfortunately all the stories were not recorded.

The communities to which the Rangers were posted have their own identities. Those posted to these diverse communities brought a commonality of training, also their own resources of common sense, fairness and personal strength of character. It is the men of the Ranger Force that make its 15-year history such a fascinating part of the Newfoundland pre-Confederation experience.

The anecdotes reported here are a small and somewhat disjointed part of the flavor of the service and the men who served as Newfoundland Rangers.

Ranger John Selby Brown kept a diary and his entry for May 2nd, 1936 reads in part: "each day had its peculiar circumstances and each village has its peculiar folk." The retelling of some of the tales more than half a century after the last day of Ranger service is an attempt to give a sense of what these men did as part of their daily work.

Common sense, Credibility and Courage

Cyril Goodyear tells the story of how in the winter of 1946-47 he was stationed as the sole Ranger in Nain, Labrador, one of the most remote communities on the coast with no access to phone and his nearest colleague 120 dog-team miles away.

One evening, Goodyear answered the door to find an hysterical middle-aged woman describing how her son-in-law, Dick Pamak, was going to kill her daughter. A second threat was made on the life of the policeman if she sought police assistance.

Dick Pamak was known as one of the best hunters in Northern Labrador, but Cyril recalls at that time the man had no friends and displayed an intimidating attitude.

Goodyear choose to leave his Smith and Wesson 38 revolver and his 303 Lee Enfield Rifle at the Ranger station and armed with only his flashlight he proceeded to the Pamak home.

It was a beautiful moonlit light and he was conscious that he was watched by someone in every home he passed enroute to the Pamak residence. He went straight to the front door and Dick Pamak opened it as he was about to knock. Dick stood with his 303 rifle pointed at Cyril's mid-section. "I have come to prevent trouble rather than cause it," stated Cyril, as he reached out and pushed the barrel of the rifle to one side.

This incident concluded with a talk on the doorstep. Dick was neither arrested nor threatened but was invited to participate in a reasoning process that worked.

Dick Pamak went on to become a fine citizen of Nain and later served as an RCMP Special Constable. In an article written in the July 1965 RCMP Quarterly, Staff Sgt. Frank Mercer, a former Ranger, told the story of how Pamik, then a 50-year-old Constable, heard the howl of dogs one stormy night and went to investigate. He found that a two man vessel had approached the wharf but because of the wind and waves was anchored offshore. Jacko Jararuse and Daniel Henock had tried to unload the wood aboard their vessel onto a float only to end up in the harbour. Jacko was lost by the time Pamak and his young son arrived on the scene and Daniel Henock, with hands frozen, was hanging onto a rope by his teeth. Launching a small boat into the wind-churned water, Panak and his son managed to locate Henock and rescue him. One can admire the courage and strength of Dick Pamak, and also the wisdom and courage of Ranger Goodyear some 17 years earlier. On that night in 1946, Goodyear rescued more than one family.

Dealing With The Problem Of Very Little

Public assistance, more commonly called the Dole, was an issue of frustration and anguish for many of the Rangers. They were charged with the front line duty of determining eligibility for the issuing or declining this financial support.

In the heart of the Great Depression of the 1930s, Ranger Ronald Peet was responsible for issuing the dole to families in Belleoram in order to prevent severe hardship. He felt if it was denied the people could riot.

He ended up being fired by the Commissioner for the Department of Public Health and Welfare because he handed out dole to those he felt needed it. The Rangers, however, were under the jurisdiction of the Department of Natural Resources and the Chief Ranger intervened on his behalf. Within hours, Public Health and Welfare acknowledged Peet's decision was correct and he was back on the job.

In another incident, the Department of Public Health and Welfare issued a directive that there was to be no able-bodied relief during the summer months. In the Placentia Bay community of St Lawrence there was very little unemployment so this was not a hardship, but at nearby Lawn there was absolutely no work. When Ranger Fagan arrived in St. Lawrence to replace Ranger Duff he was met by a delegation from Lawn and determined many people were on the edge of starvation. The result was he went ahead and issued the dole to those in need.

The Commission then changed its tactic. It had unsuccessfully attempted to fire Ranger Peet. This time, officials notified Ranger Fagan that since he had issued the relief contrary to the Directive, he would be personally responsible to repay the money.

Fagan responded by telegraphing the Commission that: "if it was the intention of the Department of Public Health and Welfare to starve the people of Lawn, then the order would be honored."

Ranger Fagan was promptly recalled to Whitbourne. Shortly afterwards, he was called to the Colonial Building in St. John's and informed that Sir John Puddester, Commissioner for the Department of Health and Welfare, wanted him fired.

He was told, however, he would not be dismissed but that he must consider himself "Dressed down" and with that reprimand he was to return to his detachment.

Ranger Fagan rightly felt that the Commission did not fully grasp the truth of circumstances in many communities. Each community had unique needs and implementing a universal policy wasn't possible.

The St. George's Rosary

Ranger Gordon Fitzpatrick of St. George's requested Ranger John Fagan of Stephenville to assist him in the arrest of four Flat Bay men believed have been stealing sheep. The evidence was so strong that FitzPatrick had provided sworn information and obtained a warrant of arrest from Magistrate Scott to bring these men into custody.

The community of Flat Bay was to the west of St. George's and inaccessible by road. Sgt. Fitzpatrick arranged to travel on an open air Newfoundland Railway Speeder to Flat Bay. The speeder would wait for the Rangers to locate the four suspects and return them to St. George's.

The arrests were made without incident and the four men went with the Rangers to the speeder and then to the cells at St. George's. The cells were located in the lowest level of the government building with the Ranger office immediately above. There were no jail guards in that particular detachment and the practice was to lock the outer doors of the building, but to leave the cell doors open so that the prisoners could keep the pot bellied stove going through the night and access the "honey buckets."

That evening, as the Rangers were preparing their reports and finishing their written work they heard a noise from below. Upon investigation, they found their four prisoners on their knees and fervently praying the Rosary.

The Shed: The loss of the SS Caribou, October 14,1942

The Caribou was a passenger and freight ferry that operated between Port aux Basques, Newfoundland, and North Sydney, Nova Scotia, beginning in the summer of 1925. During the Second World War, the Caribou carried both civilian passengers and troops, and perhaps it was the military presence that made the vessel a target for German attack.

On October 14, 1942, at 3:20 a.m. the Caribou, with 238 persons aboard, was torpedoed by a 500 tonne German U-Boat, U-69. The Caribou went down in the deepest part of the Gulf of St. Lawrence, about 25 miles southwest of Channel Head, and sank within 10 minutes. One hundred and thirty seven people perished.

The Canadian Navy sent two ships to assist in the search for survivors. As well, many small boats went out from Port aux Basques in an effort co-ordinated by Ranger Nelson Forward.

Needing help, he contacted Ranger Norman Crane who was stationed in Tompkins. Crane responded immediately.

Upon arrival, he got a small boat and went out in search of survivors and bodies but found nothing. When he returned, he found that the Bowater Paper Shed had been turned into a morgue. This shed was approximately 90 feet long and lit by three light bulbs hanging from a very high ceiling. It was generally used for storing paper from the Corner Brook mill when ice in the Bay of Islands prevented access. The shed was creepy, creaky and dark.

Ranger Clifford Caines was in charge of security at the shed and was pleased to have Crane's help. There were now twelve recovered bodies placed upon hay bundles in the shed.

Crane left to attend to other duties and when he returned he called for Caines but received no response. Crane recalls: "When Caines didn't answer I did a body count. I went through the shed with its eerie broken darkness and counted thirteen bodies. I thought I'd made a mistake so I counted again and it was still thirteen. I began the count for a third time and there in the dim light I saw a figure standing. A moment of terror! Was it a ghost?

154

"No, it was Caines! He must have been very tired in the excitement, terror and confusion of that October night to lie down among the twelve corpses."

The August 1943 Goose Bay Fire Ball Investigation

In late August 1943, Rangers George Pauls and Earl Rose with vehicle driver Jack Thevenet were working late under the direction of Ranger Art Morris. It was a peak construction period building the military base at Goose Bay, Labrador.

The Rangers were returning to base quarters sometime after 11 p.m. when they saw a "huge round ball of fire on the horizon." This fireball appeared to be to the northeast, and far out over the bay.

Morris immediately gave the order to go to the dock to arrange for a vessel to investigate. Thevenet knew one of the medium sized motor boats and its owner. In a hurry to get this skiff out to search, one of the stern lines became entangled in the propeller.

Ranger Morris acted quickly. Stripping off everything he was wearing, he dove over the side and into the cold water. He came up for air but on his second dive was successful in freeing the propeller.

Hurriedly dressing, he took the tiller, and assigned Jack Thevenet to look after the engine. Rose and Pauls were to watch for signs that could be connected to the fireball.

The search was soon underway and after what seemed a long time they observed low lying smoke coming from an island-sandbar beyond which was a glimmer of light. Uncertain of the depth of the water, they dropped anchor a safe distance away.

Sounds of shouting were soon heard followed shortly by the appearance of a small cockle shell boat with two people in it. The men aboard the shell were in RCAF uniforms and very wet. Pauls judged them to be in poor shape.

Once the men were secure on the motor boat, Ranger Rose took the shell and returned to the sandbar. The current was very swift and it was difficult to row but Rose refused help as he transported a total of fourteen men to the large skiff. As if that wasn't enough excitement, the skiff ran out of fuel as it approached land but it was close enough to be able to float ashore.

The rescued personnel explained they were aboard a Rescue Launch when a fire broke out in the engine room followed by the explosion that caused the fire ball the Rangers had seen.

President F.D. Roosevelt Writes Again

In the early morning of February 18, 1942, the U.S.S. ships Truxton and Pollux went ashore in a severe winter storm near Lawn, Placentia Bay. Two hundred and three sailors died in the disaster, but 183 were saved thanks to the help of the people of Lawn and St. Lawrence.

Ranger J. Gordon Fitzpatrick and visiting Ranger Hogan helped coordinate the rescue effort.

Within a week of the tragedy, American President Franklin Roosevelt wrote to thank the people of Lawn and St. Lawrence for what they had done.

In September of 1942, two young boys discovered a human elbow extending out of the sand on shore in Bartlett's Cove. Ranger Pauls recovered the body and it was found to be that of one of the missing American sailors, Seaman First Class F.L. Edwards from the U.S.S. Pollux.

Rev. Clench conducted a funeral service and the young seaman was buried in Ship's Cove Anglican cemetery. Shortly afterwards, Rev. Clinch received a personal letter in which President Roosevelt expressed his gratitude and that of the American people to him and Ranger Pauls.

The Sergeant's Motorcycle

Allan LeGrow was among the most capable of the remarkable men who served as Rangers. He distinguished himself as a Ranger, an RCMP officer, and a Provincial Court Judge.

Ranger LeGrow was one who followed the rules as witnessed in a story told by a former colleague and visitor to the LeGrow home.

Ranger training eventually included instruction in the operation and use of motorcycles, however Sgt. LeGrow had not received the benefit of this training either at the training depot at Whitbourne or as an inservice.

In the 1940s, however, he received a large crate containing a motorcycle for detachment use. He had the crate placed in the front room of his home and opened it there. The motorcycle remained in the front room as he learned to balance himself. It is reported that the feel of the motorcycle with engine engaged was mastered in the same room. When he felt comfortable he brought the motorcycle outside and the actual operation began. When he satisfied himself that he could operate the motorcycle, he gave himself the motorcycle test, graded himself, and issued himself a motorcycle licence.

The Importance of the Dog Licence

Ranger John Selby Brown was very sensitive to the circumstances of the people he served on the Great Northern Peninsula. It was the Dirty Thirties and times were hard. Money was a scarce commodity. The issuing and updating of various licences was the ongoing responsibility of the Ranger and Brown found himself the target of comment regarding the issuing of Dog Licences. The licence fee had to be collected or the dog destroyed. There was to be no compromise of this requirement.

Brown was a man of deep convictions and strong religious faith whose vacations included time spent at the Salvation Army "Star Lake" retreat. His memory of Ranger training at Whitbourne included "praying with the sick." He also preached on the theme of love to a Salvation Army congregation on February 21, 1936. In the final analysis, he could keep and practice his religious convictions but he had to collect the licence fees regardless of the circumstances. As told in his diary, what he did cost him his stripes and the raise in pay that accompanied them.

Excerpt from his diary August 3, 1936: I was called to the Chief's office to learn the cause of my transfer. I had been reported for not enforcing the ignoble Dog Act. (An Act requiring the licensing of all dogs at a cost of two dollars per dog, an amount which people on relief could not pay; hence their dogs must be destroyed. I had to refuse to enforce this Act many times in the North as a person's life depended entirely on a dog team). The man who reported me also stated that I spoke at Public Meetings, wearing an Army uniform. The Chief said that the authorities wanted to have me dismissed, but he would not use such drastic measures. He stated, however that I would have to forfeit my Corporal stripes. I wondered if I was dreaming, but no! I heard the Chief saying that my religious activities did not affect him, and that what I had done in that line was up to me. He said that he would stand by me and that I was not to worry. He certainly is a wonderful man. I received notice that I was to be shifted to Twillingate for a while where I won't have that dog problem.

Autopsy Photography and Jail

Thirty-year-old Benny Webb was shot to death. His body was brought to Stephenville Crossing morgue, which was located in a small building near the cottage hospital.

Ranger John Fagan was asked to assist in the murder investigation which was led by Ranger W. J. Smith with the assistance of Ranger Gordon Fitzpatrick.

Fagan recalls that by the time the body was brought to the morgue rigor mortis had taken place. Procedure required taking a picture of the corpse as evidence of the condition of the body at the time of examination. The camera was primitive and lighting was poor in the morgue. The body was stripped to show the exact location of the wound and general condition of the body. A reasonable picture was impossible in the poor light so the body was moved near a window and propped upright to get maximum natural light. The body had its right arm held up straight as the picture was snapped.

The investigation determined Benny was living with the estranged wife of John J. Young and the murder was conducted in a very deliberate fashion. Young had gone with his loaded 22 caliber rifle to what was described as the "Webb shack." He stood away from the house and threw a rock at the door. When Benny Webb opened the door, John J. Young shot him.

Young was convicted of murder and sentenced to seven years in jail.

Sgt. Fagan recalls when he later worked at the Penitentiary Young was a model prisoner and learning to read while incarcerated.

The Frozen Blanket

While stationed in Woody Point, Bonne Bay, in 1936, Ranger Vincent Nugent was required to bring a prisoner from Bonne Bay to Deer Lake for transfer to St. John's on the Newfoundland Railway. It was winter and there was no road connecting Bonne Bay and Deer Lake. Nugent arranged for a dog team and sled to transport himself and the prisoner.

The trip to Deer Lake went well but on his return the weather turned foul. It rained, it snowed, it sleeted and finally it started to freeze. Ranger Nugent found himself wet and uncomfortable on the sled and so he wrapped a blanket around him. Over the course of the trip the blanket froze solid. Nugent was helpless in the frozen blanket. He was awake, but unable to move his hand, foot, arm, or leg.

In the early morning his dog team approached Woody Point with the immobile Ranger unable to direct or control the dogs who went directly to their owners home.

The dog owners lifted the helpless Ranger like a wood log and carried him into the house where he thawed out. That incident endeared dogs to Ranger Vincent Nugent and from that day forward he declared them to be the greatest animals on this earth.

The Luggage Cart

Escort of prisoners and mental health patients was a common duty of most Rangers. Travel generally took place without incident but sometimes thing went awry. Ranger Sergeant W.J. Smith shared the story of one prisoner transport that did not go as planned.

A well known poacher of wildlife had highly refined woodsman skills which had helped him avoid arrest over a long period of time. But he was finally caught, and sentenced to six months in jail.

This man from Flat Bay was neither big nor particularly muscular in appearance. He was, however, very strong and fast and Smith reported that he was handled with care.

While some prisoners would be allowed to walk with the Ranger without handcuffs and could be instructed to stay in a particular place with confidence that those instructions would be followed, this was not the case with this man.

The time came to escort him to St. John's and the prisoner was handcuffed to Smith. He was taken to the St. George's Railway Station. Faced with a busy crowded station, Smith decided to take the prisoner behind the station and handcuff him to the building. Upon getting to the rear of the building, he saw a luggage cart 4 feet wide and 8 feet long piled high with luggage. Ranger Smith handcuffed his prisoner to the cart and checked to see the wheels were locked.

By the time he returned with the tickets he could hear the train approaching and much to his dismay, he found the cart was gone and boxes and luggage were lying all over the ground. Seeing only two ways the cart could go, he ran in that direction. As he crested a small incline he saw the empty cart and prisoner disappear at a good pace over the next incline. It took some time to catch his man and allow him to push the cart all the way back to the station. It was felt the prisoner could not have unlocked all four wheels by himself.

The next day, Ranger Smith purchased tickets before bringing his prisoner to the station, denying a repeat performance by this agile man.

Instincts Appearances and Professional Opinions

Ranger Ches Parsons was 23 years old when he was posted to Port Saunders in 1947 . During the winter a certain man exhibited difficult behavior patterns. This man would wander around the community using profane and disturbing language, make threats and generally intimidate neighbors, including his own family. He would also visit the Cottage Hospital and disrupt its general operation. He was taken into custody when his family became emotionally and physically fatigued as a consequence of his behavior. At that time there was no cell in Port Saunders in which to confine the man. Custody meant constant surveillance.

It was the view of the local Nurse and Ranger Parsons that the man was mentally ill. Certification of mental illness required agreement from two medical doctors but there were no doctors in Port Saunders.

The motor vessel Henry W. Stone put into Port Saunders on March 18, and Parsons saw this as an opportunity to take this man and obtain medical opinions with a view to certification.

Parsons boarded with his patient and the boat continued with stops at Flowers Cove and then on to Port aux Basques where a doctor examined the man. He was suddenly acting so reasonable the doctor questioned whether certification was appropriate.

Parsons continued by taking the train to Corner Brook. Again, the man's behavior was reasonable in the presence of a doctor, but away from observation he was as disturbed as ever. It was the same story as Parsons visited other doctors in the area.

Parsons continued on his way back to Woody Point in Bonne Bay. He learned the man had relatives nearby and they agreed to accommodate him for the night. But the Ranger had just arrived at his boarding house when the relatives called to withdraw their offer as the man was cursing up a storm. Ranger Parsons took him back in custody and put him in a jail cell for the night.

The frustrating search continued the next day with a trip across Bonne Bay to Dr. Noel Murphy but still no certification was forthcoming.

Nothing left to do but return to Port Saunders. This was not an easy trip in late March in the company of a man Dr. Murphy felt to be borderline.

The trip covered approximately 700 miles and took 12 days. Ranger Force head office was budget conscious and Ranger Parsons recalls he was brought to task by way of a memorandum.

The man eventually did some malicious damage. Charges were laid and he was sentenced to three months in jail where his behaviour was monitored and resulted in him being committed to the Mental Hospital from which he was never released.

Ches Parsons still remembers the rebuke he received for failing to get the man certified. But the end result showed that his efforts were correct and that this poor man from Port Saunders required more medical attention than was available in 1947.

Jack Fagan Recalls A Sad Story

I was on patrol on the Port au Port Peninsula when some people came to me and reported that a young fellow had been out in a boat with his brother-in-law, and the brother-in-law reached for a shotgun to shoot a bird, and the gun went off as he was pulling it towards him. The young fellow, a twelve-year-old boy, was rowing and the full blast of the twelve-gauge shotgun hit him in the leg. It actually severed the leg.

So I went up to the house, and they had the young fellow laid on a tarpaulin in the kitchen. He was conscious but he was in shock, and bleeding very badly. So I put a tourniquet on the leg, and left instructions with the people there to loosen it every few minutes and tighten it again. Then, I went to the nearest phone by horse and buggy and phoned the American hospital at Stephenville. I asked them to send an ambulance to the other side of the bay where there was a road and I'd try to get over by boat. But when I went back, the boy was dead.

This Was My Ranger, by Margaret (Ball) Saunders

Lloyd Saunders was born in Carbonear on July 26,1915, the son of Ursula (Clark) and William Saunders. His father owned the local cooperage shop, where as a boy Lloyd often worked and helped out, making barrels for the purpose of shipping capelin and salt fish to foreign markets.

He attended Carbonear Academy and grew up participating in all the common activities that young boys at that age were interested in - skating, hockey, football, weight lifting and trout-fishing. He attended Sunday school, went on picnics, went to movies, and also was a great boxer.

In 1933, at the age of 16, he embarked on the Kyle and set sail for Labrador to work with the Hudson's Bay Company where he spent the next 5 years of his life as a clerk in their store.

He went back home to Carbonear in 1938 - a period of time in our history when poverty and unemployment were almost the order of the day. The Commission of Government had just started a new organization - THE NEWFOUNDLAND RANGERS - to look into the problems facing our country, so jobs being scarce, Lloyd applied for a position with them. He accepted and on the 5th of May 1939, he became a 1st Class Ranger with the Regimental Number of 73. He would remain with the Rangers until the Force was disbanded in 1950 when he transferred to the RCMP.

After completing his training at Whitbourne, he was posted again to Labrador, and served in the small outposts along the coast - Makkovik, Rigolet, Davis Inlet, Rankin Inlet, and Nain. After serving in Labrador, he was sent to Grand Bank and Belleoram, then to Norris Arm and finally to Badger, where he met and married yours truly - Margaret Ball - and remained there until the RCMP took over the Force in 1950, when he was sent to Grand Falls where he resided until his death on November 12, 1992.

What was there about Labrador that fascinated him so? He never tired of talking about that great land, and the stories he told would fill a good-sized volume - if I could remember them all. Whether they were true or not is another matter!

He developed a high regard for the people he lived and worked with - The Masseys, the Andersens, the Christians, the Moravian Missionaries (Rev. Hetesh and daughter Kate) and the native people, besides his own colleagues and co-workers - Strickland, Howard, Mercer, English, Rockwood - and many, many more whose names I can no longer remember.

This was over 60 years ago, and in those days there was no such thing as a radio, no telephones, no walkie-talkies, no TV, no highways, no sleek police cars, no fancy snowmobiles or ATV's, no helicopters or bush planes. Your only means of transportation was on foot, or snowshoes, by dog-team or by motor-boat. Your only means of communication with the outside world was by the coastal boat that went back and forth until everything was frozen up early in winter.

Can you imagine a young fellow of today having to live and work in such conditions? It would be unheard of! Just think about Howard and himself having to live off tin soup all winter long because the supply boat didn't arrive on time before freeze-up, having to write reports with frozen ink; or in the case of English - becoming separated from his dog team, left wandering around the frozen lake - snow-blind, luckily being rescued later on, or being lost in a raging snow storm, and being found by a couple of natives, and having to live in a tent for 10 days until the storm abated.

What breed of men were they to survive the endless obstacles they faced day after day!

Out of all the stories Lloyd used to tell about when he lived and worked in Labrador, one in particular stands out in my memory. While stationed in Nain, there was a mining prospector who used to go to Labrador in search of minerals. Of course in those days there was no such thing as the great drilling machines of today, or helicopters or airplanes. All such ventures had to be undertaken on foot. This prospector would arrive with his little pickaxe and shovel, go to the local store and get a supply of provisions- flour, tea, sugar, milk, molasses, etc. Then with his knapsack full he would take off in the bush, hopefully to discover his fortune.

Day after day went by, then weeks and no sign of the prospector's returning. Lloyd had just about given him up for lost and was on the point of getting a search party together to look for him when lo and behold he arrived back in the settlement safe and sound. He was hardly recognizable as the same man that had left - hair almost shoulder-length, five or six week's of beard, chewed to pieces from the flies. All provisions gone. But - a knapsack full of rocks.

Turning up in Lloyd's office he excitedly related his adventures, telling about the wonderful discovery he had found. Taking each rock out of his knapsack and placing it lovingly on the desk, he pointed out to Lloyd what the different markings meant, so that even Lloyd - in his ignorance of such matters - was impressed by the find. "Ranger Boy," the prospector kept saying, "there's somethin' there, somethin' big there send this off and have it analyzed."

Lloyd dutifully packaged the prospector's find and sent it to the Department of Mines and Resources in St. John's, hoping Delaney wouldn't hear about it, and wonder if #73 had suddenly developed rocks in his head. Lloyd never did say the name of the prospector.

Shortly thereafter Lloyd was transferred from Nain to Grand Bank. By this time the war was upon us, and whatever the analysis of the prospector's rocks turned out to be nothing more was heard of the matter.

During recent years with all the interest being shown in mineral exploration and all the drilling going on in the province - I have often thought back on the story Lloyd used to tell about the prospector and his rocks , and wonder to myself: could this have been the beginning of our great Voisey's Bay?

The Rabbit Pie

Mary Kelloway Smith was married to Ranger William J. Smith d they both knew Ranger John Hogan. She recalled the sadness during the time that Hogan was missing after he parachuted out of a plane on the Northern Peninsula. She spoke of the exhilaration that swept through the ranks of the Ranger Force when it was discovered that Hogan had survived his fifty days in the wilderness. It was a cause of celebration.

When the first opportunity presented itself, Mary Smith undertook to prepare a special meal for now Ranger Corporal Hogan of Deer Lake.

Mary told the story of how she asked her husband what was Corporal Hogan's favourite meal.

She was informed that Baked Rabbit Casserole with a thick Pastry Crust was always his preferred meal. She had never made a rabbit casserole before. She had no rabbits and no recipe. She had little trouble locating a recipe. The rabbit, however, was a different story. She arranged for a young hunter to trap and sell her a brace (two) of rabbits.

The rabbits were delivered unskinned with head and feet still intact. Mary had previously purchased chickens for Sunday dinner that were brought to the door live and squawking. The same people who had prepared the chickens for cooking were also experienced with rabbits so off she trotted with the rabbits in hand.

She then prepared the Rabbit Casserole and followed up with baking an assortment of home baked cookies as well as an apple pie and her specialty lemon pie. Her husband arranged for a bottle of rum from the Corner Brook Liquor Store. They were prepared to celebrate with Ranger Hogan.

But fifty days in the wilderness had changed Ranger Hogan's diet preferences. The aroma of the rabbits Mary had so lovingly prepared permeated the Ranger quarters. For Hogan, it was a sickening reminder of the ten rabbits he had lived on during his fifty days in the Great Northern Peninsula wilderness. The party ended up being relocated while the windows were opened to clean out the rabbit smell. An alternative menu was quickly devised and enjoyed

The Wreck of the Sabina Airliner

Ranger Fred Davis recalled the biggest job of his career was the Sabina Airplane crash.

The plane had been down for three days before she was even found, because no one knew just where the crash had occurred – somewhere within a radius of thirty miles. Everything was fogged in, and the plane was coming in on ground control approach when she disappeared off the radar screen.

When we got there, up on the southwest Gander River, everything was still soaking wet from rain and fog, and bodies were lying on the ground all over the place, all soaking wet. There were a lot of survivors from the crash. One of them was a young Chinese doctor, and he was the real hero of that accident. He'd spent the whole three days working on the survivors although he had no equipment. There were eighteen people living when we got to the site, but one of them died afterwards, so the total was actually seventeen survivors, and this young doctor, with two or three years of medical school, looked after them, treating them for fractured limbs and shock and so on. He had some cuts – one gash that took eight or ten stitches, I think, and his face and neck cut up a bit, with blood dried black when I first saw him. But even though he had no equipment he improvised splints and so on, and patched people up, and saved all but one of them. He'd made a shelter from parts of the aircraft, and was still working, without sleep, into his fourth day when I arrived there at the head of a party of twenty-five men.

The way we found the wreck was this: a crew came in from Argentia with a helicopter, and they knew the general area where the airplane disappeared. Then they flew around and got a magnetic contact that turned out to be the wreck near Dead Wolf Brook, about three miles from Caribou Pond.

There were twenty-seven bodies. I took the wireless operator down out of a birch tree, where he was draped across a limb, twenty feet or more off the ground, just like a piece of cloth, with the earphones still on his head, and five or six feet of wire.

I picked up pieces of bodies, limbs and so on, part of a fellow's head stuck on a tree. You get used to that kind of thing. I'd worked in the paper mill in Grand Falls and I saw several men killed on the job. First time it's horrible, but after that there's nothing to it. Familiarity, you see. The plane had caught fire and some of the bodies burned so there were only parts of them left. From the waist up it might all be beautiful pink flesh, still sitting in a seat, and the legs all burned away, not even cinders left.

There were suitcases up in trees, too, because she'd come down on a slant, sheared off the trees, torn open the fuselage, and there was luggage scattered everywhere.

The bodies were all lying around for five days before they were buried and it was summer. They dropped a radio to me so I could talk with the planes as they flew overhead, and I asked Gander what they wanted to do with the bodies. I was advised it was too risky to carry them out as you'd need eight men to a stretcher, working in relays in that rough country.

So they decided to bury them there. They started a cemetery, a graveyard named St. Martin of the Woods, and we buried twenty-seven of them there in the country. We had to lay out the bodies and search them and take the valuables off them and tag them – and after so long, there, there were flies, and the bodies were starting to decay – terrible work – so I radioed Gander for two cases of Hudson Bay rum, and they dropped them to me, and we drank rum until we could handle the bodies without getting sick – we had to get three parts shot to handle them because some of the bodies were putrefied by then.

They flew in a Canso amphibian plane to Caribou Pond, and the survivors were lifted by helicopter to the pond, and flew them out.

Well, I got a citation for the work, and a platinum cigarette lighter from the Belgium government, but I said I wouldn't take it unless all twenty-five men in the party got the same thing. They'd all done the same work, they had to handle the bodies, dig the graves and bury them.

Much later, a few of the bodies were moved back to Belgium but that was several years later.

Among the things we took from the bodies was money. I had 22,000 American dollars drying out in a warming closet of my stove in Glenwood when I got back. The stuff was wringing wet, soaked by the rain. They believed that there was some smuggling going on, because the money was taken off the bodies of the crew of the aircraft, and 22,000 American dollars was one hell of a lot of money back in those days.

Robert Smith's Two Youthful Memories of RCMP Officer John Hogan

In June 2003, at age 57, while I was in Deer Lake to attend a funeral of a friend, I walked into the coffee room of a funeral parlor. There was a collection of men seated around a table. They all looked to be about my age or older. I knew none of these men nor their names.

It was now almost 50 years ago since RCMP Corporal John Hogan had held me tight on a railway platform in Deer Lake to prevent me running toward a moving train. I wondered if any of these men remembered him. Even as I impulsively spoke, I thought they would have been too young to remember a man gone from their community since the 1950's.

The men surprised me with a little chorus of "Oh yes!" One man said, " He was a great man, how could you forget Officer Hogan?" I asked for details of this man's experience with Corporal Hogan and he slowly replied he had none. When I asked the root of Hogan's greatness , there was no clear response. One man said: "He was fair and tough." No prodding of these men could bring an answer because that was all they knew. Corporal John Hogan had served as an RCMP officer in Deer Lake. He was highly regarded but the roots of that reputation were lost among these men. Only the conclusion of greatness remained.

In mid-December1953 I was seven years old. Mom had a new baby, a sister for me. Our family of four was moving from St. John's to Corner Brook. We traveled on the Newfoundland Railway. The train stopped in Deer Lake in the winter dark. We all got off for what purpose I wasn't sure. I knew we were not in Corner Brook and this place had no context or meaning for me. There were people all over the platform, some talking, some struggling with luggage, some just standing there doing apparently nothing but waiting, and others greeting each other or saying goodbye.

Within seconds, a uniformed RCMP officer appeared. He was a big man with a moustache who seemed to know my Mom and Dad. He spoke to us all. He bent down and asked how was I enjoying the long ride from St. John's and was I looking forward to a new school in Corner Brook? I was surprised by his interest. I wasn't sure I was too comfortable with this man I had never met before. His interest in me was more than I usually attracted from adults who by and large ignored me. Dad said Corporal

Hogan was a very special friend who had come to greet us as we moved to our new home in Corner Brook.

It seemed Mom and Dad and this man talked for a long time. I just wanted to get back on the train and get to Corner Brook. I was not paying any particular attention to what was happening when all of a sudden, Dad said, "Robert, you stay with Corporal Hogan!"

"What? Why?" I spoke out loud. Mom and Dad started down the platform towards the train. I started after them. Corporal Hogan grabbed my arm as he said, "No, Robert, your Mom and Dad will be back in a second. You are to wait with me."

In panic, I watched as Mom and Dad boarded the train. Corporal Hogan was talking about Mom and Dad. He was very friendly. I did not like this situation. This big man was still holding my arm, although not as firmly. I said, "It's alright, I'm going back on the train." I then bolted for the train. As I started to run, the train started to move. Corporal Hogan grabbed the back of my jacket. The train was moving. I was going to Corner Brook but now I was being left with this man. There was the whistle, there was significant movement of the train as it moved up the tracks. I screamed, "I want to go with Mom and Dad." I was sure this was it, I would never see them again.

Corporal Hogan was talking and trying hard to reassure me that Mom and Dad had not left but would be back in just a few minutes. I was crying and could see the train still moving. I wasn't listening to what he was saying, I was screaming. I stopped crying for a second and he tried to readjust his grip. I again tried to bolt. The train was now way up the tracks but it had stopped. Corporal Hogan took me in his arms. I was crying and screaming, and he held me and spoke. I could see the train now fully stopped. Maybe if I were too difficult, he would give me back, I thought. I yelled and squirmed, and struggled to no avail. When I pleaded with people standing nearby they turned away from me.

All of a sudden, it was clear, the train was returning. The Corporal was right. Within minutes the train was back to almost the exact spot from which it had left. I felt better and now his holding me in his arms seemed reassuring as opposed to the threat it posed only moments before. Within moments Dad was off the train. There were goodbyes and I was back on the train.

I have always felt a little embarrassed about my behavior as a seven year old on that railway platform. It was only me, Corporal Hogan, and all the people on the railway platform that knew. Mom and Dad never mentioned it. Or maybe I was so relieved to get on the train, I just don't remember.

If I thought I had seen the end of Corporal Hogan, I was wrong. At first, life in Corner Brook was without a car. Every now and then Dad rented an old used car from the Star Taxi. When there was talk of renting one, I knew what was in store. It would be a trip to Deer Lake. There would be five miles of pavement and twenty miles of bumps and plenty of dust. The Hogans had two girls about my age and a boy just a little younger than me. They had a card table that folded, with a checker board printed on the table itself. They had board games and toys that were different than mine. This was the excitement of Deer Lake and I was always anxious to get there.

Not only that, but they all lived in an RCMP Station. There were jail cells, real jail cells. There were handcuffs, and real revolvers. There were real "Wanted posters."

In the beginning, I only heard of what was below the Hogans living quarters. I had never seen the inside of a police station. It was there. It was real. It was the stories I savored.

One evening we visited the Hogans in the middle of an Autumn school week. I don't know how it happened but we visited at a inconvenient time when there was a lot of homework to be done. Maybe Dad wanted to consult with the Corporal, and this was the only time. While the Hogan children did homework I was seated alone in the living room and treated to cookies, cake, and juice. Eventually the adults joined me. There was another conversation that had no meaning for me. I was disappointed about no play companions. Then, I leaned over to ask Dad if I could see the jail. Dad hushed me. Corporal Hogan overheard and said that there was no person being detained at that time in the cells, no officer on duty and that he would be pleased to give a tour. I was going to visit a real jail cell!

Corporal Hogan showed me handcuffs. "Let me try them on?" I begged and he did, as well as explaining the use of handcuffs and letting me handcuff him in order to demonstrate how difficult they were to unlock. He also put me in a cell but didn't lock the door. Back in his office he took a 50-page clipboard off the wall and showed me that each page was a wanted bulletin with usually a photograph and some information on the person wanted. It was always men, never women, in the bulletins I saw. I was also shown a revolver and holster and ammunition. This was a look but do not touch situation. The memory of that forty-five minutes has lasted all my life.

On the next visit Corporal Hogan answered the door and his first words were directed at me, "Robert, we have some important business. New wanted bulletins have been received. We have to review them. Another set of eyes on the watch for these dangerous men would be helpful." So off we went to the police office. Corporal Hogan and I had progressed a long way from the December 1953 railway platform. The Corporal had earned a fan for life.

Amateur Doctor By Ranger Ferdinand Davis

In those days there were few roads. You had to walk in winter and take a boat in summer. In winter you'd pack a bag with clothes, extra underwear and socks and so on, and take as much food as you could , a walk, say, from LaScie to Baie Vert - that was about thirty-five miles - think nothing of it - walk back.

You'd take a sleeping bag with you and walk on snowshoes. Walking down the road for thirty-five miles is a pretty fair jaunt, but much easier than with snowshoes on. Sometimes, you know a snowstorm would come up, and you'd have to make a tent—what they call a bough whiffen, to protect you from the elements, and get into your sleeping bag – but it was pretty rough going sometimes.

And sometimes you could stay at a house, but a lot of people didn't even have a pan to bake a bun of bread. They'd mix the dough and put it on the damper of the stove. They used to call them damper downs.

Every fall they used to send me a steel drum with forty-five gallons of cod liver oil, and they'd send me fifteen or twenty cases of Coco-malt, in gallon cans like paint tins, and I'd have to distribute it to the schools with instructions to the teachers. Every day at recess each child was to receive a tablespoonful of cod liver oil. And all the kids had to have mugs with their manes on them – pieces of sticking plaster on the bottoms of the mugs, with the names, to have their mug of Coco-malt. Quite often the kids were too poor to buy a mug, so I had to buy one.

This was to help combat malnutrition – tuberculosis and beri-beri, which was very common then. I really hated that bloody Coco-malt, because I had to drink the stuff every time I visited a school, to make a good impression on the kids and the teacher, to convince them that the stuff wasn't poison, you know.

I helped people to get kidney and liver pills and cod liver oil and all that kind of stuff – junk, most of it, but you'd be amazed the number of people who had faith in it – they heard about it on the Doyle News on the radio every night – and sure enough, you'd get the pills for them and they'd take a couple and it would be, "Oh, the finest kind now, sir." And so they would be, because about eighty percent of disease is psychological. Nobody has a toothache as bad as they think they have. I pulled hundreds of teeth.

I had two pairs of forceps, and they'd come and sit in a chair in my office, women as well as men, and I'd pull away. Sometimes their jaws would be swollen, and I'd pull their teeth anyway – I didn't know the difference, you see.

One time Bob Jackman, a fellow from Tilt Cove, came over. He had a lot of gold on his teeth, done in England. Big scarf wrapped around his face, all swollen up, and I said, "What happened, boy," and he said, "I had a toothache – no toothache now, but me face been swollen like this around two weeks."

He didn't tell me that he'd hired a boat and gone to Twillingate, and that Dr. Olds had sent him home again, refusing to pull the tooth until the swelling went down. So I got him in the chair, and propped his mouth open with a piece of wood – three-quarter-inch wood, so I could keep it open to see the teeth – and I got a tooth out, and all the corruption came after it..... Dr. Olds cursed me up the clouds. "How he didn't die is beyond me," the Doctor said. "What kind of a fool are you anyway?"`

Well, fools rush in where doctors fear to tread, you know, and this time it worked out alright, as it happened. Besides the forceps I had a booklet about the symptoms of simple medical problems – supplied by the Department of Health. I also had a big jar of Saunders' Mixture for upset stomach, and codeine tablets – you need a prescription for those – I had bloody great big boxes of them, and used them much as you'd use aspirin today.

Of course I'd been given a course in first aid, and a little better than first aid, by Dr. Cluny MacPherson. It was a bit beyond first aid, because we were supplied with needles and catgut for sewing up cuts, and that kind of minor surgery, you know. I often took hooks out of fishermen's hands, and bits of bone, and stuff like that.

For antiseptic, I used Epsom Salts in water as hot as you could bear with your finger.

Over on the west coast one time I was caught trying to get a woman to the hospital. She was expecting, you know, and the baby was born in the car. I got the mother and baby to Corner Brook hospital, to Dr. Cochrane, and the nurse came out and took the child and someone with a stretcher, and took the woman, and everything worked out just fine.

One time at Cox's Cove I was helping with a search for goods taken from a wreck, and a woman came out of her house saying, "oh my God, come in, sir. Priscilla is dying." When I went in the house first thing I saw was this poor girl, stretched out on a couch in the kitchen without a stitch on, covered with blood and tar.

What had happened was that a number of grapnels, fresh from the forge, coated with tar, had been placed at the head of the wharf, and she had gone in the dark and fell among them. One of the points of the grapnels had gone into her right breast, and we couldn't tell how bad she was – it really looked like she might be dying, with all that tar and blood.

So I sent for a woman from next door to help, and she happened to be a midwife. First we had to get the tar off, with hot water, and I used a handful of salt for antiseptic. And after we had her cleaned up, she moaning and groaning all the while, the woman said, "We'll have to try to stitch up the gash in her breast. There's no way we can get her to hospital tonight."

We were about twenty-two miles from Corner Brook, by boat. There was no road, and though the weather was clear, it was blowing a gale, and you'd never get there in a small boat. So between this old lady and myself, we sewed the young woman up with white sewing cotton.

It was four days later that they got her into the hospital at Corner Brook, to the same doctor – Dr. Cochrane – and he said, "when you get back to him, now, you tell him in three days time to take the stitches out."

So I cut the stitches and took them out and later when I visited the place again, her mother saw me and called me in to see how perfectly the wound had healed.

Taken from Ranger Bulletin No. 6 (1943)

COURTESY IS THE BEST POLICY

To be a real policeman
Be big and strong by heck
But let the strength be always found
Just above the neck.

By this I really do not mean
A great big husky throat
To bawl some poor old victim out
And make of him a goat

But brain inspired carry on
To see your duty through
And do unto your victim
As you'd have him do to you

Don't think that just a uniform
Or a badge upon your vest
Will make of you an officer
Or help you stand the test

It takes a lot of patience
Cool headedness as well
A touch or two of courtesy
The results then soon will tell

Remember that your buddy
As well as all the Force
Will be judged by your lone action
So choose the better course

Then when your job is ended
And your services are through
They'll say it's a fine Department
And all because of you

Ranger Rex Dingwall Recalls taking Mental Patients to St. John's

We had to travel thirty miles by horse to Port au Port, then eighteen miles more to Stephenville Crossing to get a train, then up to the Gaff Topsails, stuck there for two days. The escort lady would be there, and the patient there, and I'd be sitting up front; she wasn't in a straight jacket or anything, she wasn't violent, but one time she decided to come and sit on my lap, and she left her trademark.... another time, with an old gentleman, a male patient, driving in through Port au Port I thought he might be hungry as we'd come quite a few miles, so I went in to Haliburton's store and bought some bananas, but instead of eating his banana he peeled it and smeared it all over my face.

I was called to go to the peninsula, where there was a man who had turned the whole family out of the house, and was in the kitchen with a knife – a large fish knife – refusing to allow anyone to enter
It took me some hours to get there, by boat and then by foot, and they told me he was still inside, pointing out the house. It took a lot of nerve to go in, but I couldn't back down because then I'd be really laughed at – the Ranger afraid to face the man – so I just very cautiously went into the house, keeping alert and my eyes open, and sure enough there he was, standing up with the knife in his hands. So I just pounced on him, and the knife dropped, and I took him in to the mental hospital.

Hebron 1946

Ranger Ches Parsons was 21 when he completed his basic training in Kilbride. He spent six months in Lamaline, on the Burin Peninsula, and was then reassigned to the remote northern Labrador community of Hebron. Ranger Parsons was raised on Bell Island, Conception Bay, and unfamiliar with the idiosyncracies of life in the far north. He arrived to find the station had been closed for a few months as was the custom. He'd had no orientation to this posting.

Hebron was a community of 120 people, 110 of them Inuit who spoke no English and had a primitive lifestyle. The community had a Moravian Mission and a government store, which had been formerly owned and operated by the Hudson Bay Company. While the policing needs of Hebron were minimal, the social needs, food requirements, and medical necessities had to be carefully assessed and monitored .

During February, the manager of the government store advised that supplies of ammunition were running low and there was a danger that during March the supply would be depleted. This meant that the government relief rolls would swell and questions would be forthcoming. Ranger Parsons, now 22, was a problem solver. An enquiry to the Nain government store indicated that supplies of ammunition were available there. The alternative action would have been a patrol to Chimo in Canada, then a foreign country.

The 380 mile return trip to Nain meant going over the Kiglapait Mountains, not once but twice. The Kiglapaits are known by the Inuit as the "dog toothed mountains," a description which suggests the jagged and steep nature of the mountain. This coastal range, 900 meters high, is located 50 miles north of Nain. It is challenging not only because of the steepness and roughness of the rock but also because it is exposed to winds that sweep in from the ocean.

A Cape Chidley Inuit, Simeon Jararuse, who did not speak English, agreed to guide Ranger Parsons on his supply gathering trip to Nain. They set out with extra clothing and sufficient food for themselves and their dogs.

It took four days to reach Nain. The most difficult challenge was the mountain which required them to walk up the slopes ahead of the dogs in order to blaze the trail. The snow, which had drifted down through the trees, had a fluffy texture which hindered the dogs from pulling the sled. The snow was often over the heads of the dogs. At times, Parsons and the guide were up to their armpits in snow. The winding trek up the Kiglapaits was the most exhausting part of the fourteen day journey. The more than 2,700 foot climb took seven hours. Ranger Parsons recalls that the guide and he were lost on the mountain top four times as they searched for a route down to the shore line.

Attaining the summit is always exhilarating but on this trip it did not mean the end of difficulties. Ranger Parsons and the guide decided to leave the dogs in harness as they descended, a decision which meant the steep slope of the mountains took control. A dog was lost when the sled hit "ballicaters." The"ballicaters" were at the base of the slopes where the sea water hit the rocky shoreline and froze. The collision with ice caused the sled runners to break. The two men repaired the runners and grub box with sealskin line.

Along the shoreline another dog was lost when it went through the ice and had to be cut loose. A snow storm put the lives of the men at risk. Jararuse found his way through the storm by running along the shoreline and keeping the mountains in sight. This strategy worked and kept them on track to Nain.

At about 7 p.m. that evening they came upon an Inuit hut. The half dozen people camped there welcomed them. They stayed overnight and the next day borrowed a number of dogs to help them continue on to Nain.

On the fourth day they arrived in Nain and were welcomed by Cyril Goodyear, the Ranger in charge. Two days later, with their sled heavily loaded with ammunition and other provisions, they began their return to Hebron.

At the top of the Kiglapait mountains they were caught in a snow storm and were forced to make a small igloo (snow house) where they were trapped for three days.

When they reached the cabin at Nutak, a stopping off place at the base of the mountain, Ranger Parsons used his pocket knife to carve fourteen words into a log in the cabin.

During this trip Parsons was frostbitten on five occasions. At times the only way to keep warm was to run with the dogs. The exhaustion was intense and difficult to put into exact words. The trip lasted fourteen days, one day for every word Ranger Parsons carved into the log in Nutak.

They finally arrived safely back in Hebron with the ammunition.

In 1947, Ranger William Mullaly replaced Parsons at Hebron. Years later he asked Parsons if he remembered what he had written on that log in Nutak on his return journey. Parsons had forgotten but Mullaly had not, and he recited, "I don't have to go to hell any more, I have already been there."

DIARY OF NEWFOUNDLAND RANGER HOGAN

The following are actual excerpts from Ranger Hogan's diary after a perceived fire aboard an Air Force plane enroute from Goose Bay to Gander led him and two other passengers to bail out over the Northern Peninsula of Newfoundland on May 8, 1943.

Saturday May 8,th 1943

Left Goose 3:15 p.m. in Ventura AJ164. Bailed out approximately at 4: 45 p.m., presumably over Newfoundland and lander on frozen pond, injured knee. Two parachuted before me, namely, Corporal Butt and one other. First night slept in tent made from parachute, weather rainy and foggy.

Sunday May 9th

At dawn decided to walk to coast, as I saw an island. About 11:00 a.m. overtook Cpl. Butt who was also making for the coast. We walked all day and camped at 6:00 p.m. No food. Butt, who lost flying boots in fall, finds his feet becoming numb with the cold. Cooked a rabbit which I picked up. Weather cold and windy. Slept on bows and kept fire going all night.

Monday May 10th

Started walking at 5:00 a.m. no food. Butt finding ankle, which he sprained in landing, bothering him. Camped at 6:00 p.m.

Tuesday, May 11th

Started over river route again. Ate some browse and cane, drinking plenty of water from brooks and ponds. In the evening found a rabbit in snare left by trappers. Ate one half of it for tea. First food since Sunday. Camped at 6:15 p.m. Both our feet in bad condition, but feeling good and hoping to get to coast in a day or two. A little rain during the day.

Wednesday, May 12th

Started at 7:00 a.m. to walk around point of woods but returned. Ate the second half of our rabbit. Butt's feet badly frostbitten and shoes practically gone. Camped at 1:00 p.m. to give Butt a chance to rest.

Thursday. May 13th

Broke camp at 7:00 a.m. after spending cold night sleeping on bows in the bush. Plane passed overhead on Wednesday at 3:45 p.m. but did not see us or smoke from fire which we had burning.

Friday, May 14th
Broke camp at 8:30 after a very cold night, and walked around pond all day. Picked up a few berries on marshes. Weather blowing hard but sunshiny.

Saturday, May 15th
Broke camp at 7:30 a.m. Living on leaves and water. Butt's feet very worn and blistered. Half hour after breaking camp, ran into log cabin at end of pond and found there small piece of pork which we took and ate. Struck a river at 9:30 a.m. and followed same all day, moving very slowly as Butt's feet very sore. Camped at 5:00 p.m. and had a very cold night. No sleep. Shifted at 5:00 a.m. to a dryer spot.

Sunday, May 16th
Broke camp at 7:30 a.m. and started off. No food, only leaves. Came to a large pond where pulpwood had washed ashore. Reached old camp site at 3:00 p.m. Camped here overnight by building a lean-to behind an old camp, only it caught fire at 2:30 a.m. and we had to scramble, spoiled night's rest.

Monday, May 17th
Broke camp at 6:30 a.m. Walked around pond which I thought to be Blue Pond, or Westbrooke Pond, to find a river running into Hawke's Bay. This pond has large arms. Weather becoming showery at 10:00 a.m. and rain at noon. At 3;00 p.m. reached trapper's camp where we found a half loaf of bread and a small piece of salt fish. Picked up some wood and made a shelter for the night. Up to now we had eaten leaves and buds from young trees and found them strengthening.

Tuesday, May 18th
Remained in camp all day as wet snow falling. Had to burn trapper's boats and some of his camp materials.

Wednesday, May 19th
Broke camp at 8:30 a.m. Butt decided to remain at camp while I go for aid, but I returned at 10:30 a.m., failing to cross river to opposite side. Living on browse and water.

Thursday, May 20th
Both of us left at 9:00 a.m. to walk around pond. Found distance too long and decided to return to camp. Returning found a rabbit which was fresh and which we ate. Remained at camp all day.

Friday, May 21st
Had a fair night. Fire kept in all night. Proposed to make a raft to cross pond but failed to do so as we were too weak. Made a stew of rabbit bones and paws in a tin can. In the evening set four rabbit snares.

Saturday, May 22nd
Went to snares in morning, but no rabbits. We have now to remain around camp and wait for water to subside. Butt feeling weak; his feet very sore.

Sunday, May 23rd
Found one rabbit in snare this morning. Roasted same and made broth from bones in tomato can. Remained at camp most of time to gather wood for fire which has been kept going constantly owing to only having six matches left. Feeling pretty well myself.

Monday, May 24th
Went to snare, but no rabbit. Dressed Butt's feet in the evening. Cut wood. Ate browse and drank water. Fixed up snares in the evening.

Tuesday, May 25th
Caught two rabbits today. Ate one and kept one for tomorrow. Fine weather. Both feeling a little exhausted after eating.

Wednesday, May 26th
Caught no rabbits this morning. Ate remainder rabbit from yesterday and leaves. Fixed snares and gathered wood. Decided to cross river tomorrow, if fine day.

Thursday, May 27th
Caught one rabbit this morning. Ate same. Attempted at 1:00 p.m. to cross river but current too strong; almost swept us off our feet. Butt's feet in very poor condition.

From Friday May 28th until Thursday June 24th Hogan and Butt remained at the cabin. They gathered firewood to keep a fire going, set snares for rabbits, and gathered greens from early growth to augment their diet. During this period they caught only six rabbits.

Friday, June 25th 1943
Usual chores. At 2:30 p.m. two dories appeared near our camp with three members of survey party, namely: Francis Perry of Port Saunders; Wm. Lawrence of Port aux Basque; John H. Parsons of Parsons Pond. These Newfoundlander were our rescuers who revived us with food.

Saturday, June 26th

At 8:50 a.m. our rescuing party took us to Hawk's Bay. From there Bowaters Ltd. conveyed us by motor boat to Port Saunders where we arrived at 5:50 p.m., and at 10:15 p.m. Group Captain Anderson of the Royal Air Force Transport Command unit, Gander, arrived by Norseman with a doctor who pronounced us as being fit for air travel next day.

Sunday, June 27th

About 2:15 p.m. We left Port Saunders and arrived at Gander at 4:15.

Our ordeal was over.

Excerpt from diary of Ranger George Pauls on Friday, September 18, 1936. At the time he was stationed in Twillingate.

This evening I saw one of the most beautiful sunsets that I have ever witnessed. The sun sank beyond a becalmed sea which gleamed a silver blue except for the rare purple of its rippled currents. On the western sky there gleamed gold, purple and unusual tints of pale green. A wisp of cooud floated over the sea and caught the luminous ray of the sun its its borders. It glowed in a reddish tinge and deepened to crimson gleam. Soon it became an island of scarlet in the tranquil air. A murkish purple cloud hung low over the far away mainland, and trailed away to the blue infinity of the east. In this cloud the crescent of the new moon hung like a golden bow aimed toward the departing sun. The only sound to greet my ears was the low murmuring swish of the sea as it played about the beach. I turned my back to the sunset and gazed toward the east. There the blue of the approaching night dwelt in fathomless beauty. This was a colour that seemed altogether different from any other that greeted the eye. Instead of having a solid appearance, that is of being tangible or material, it was lost in infinite space. One tried to look beyond this blue, into it as it were, to find a base. Overhead the clouds were adorned with modest beauty. There was no colourful brillance but a subdued splendour of pale golds, greys, blues and pinks. It gave one the thrill of being alive, and it inspired heartfelt thanks for manifold blessings. It seemed incredible in this evening's charm that death and destruction were working its horrors in the Civil War in Spain, or that they were also reaping their sheaves in the storms to the south of us. Wars and hurricanes. death and destruction were rampant in other countries. But here were becalmed waters, evening splendour and contentment. We love thee Newfoundland. ...How many in hospital, the fishing boat, on the battlefield or the street, under bondage or tormented by fear would gladly exchange places with me. How many with wealth, high position and fame would gladly sacrifice it all for my peace of mind.

The following is an editorial that was widely reprinted throughout the province following the Ranger Force being replaced by the RCMP on July 27, 1950. Quoted by Harold Horwood in his book, A History of the Newfoundland Ranger Force, it well expresses the high regard in which people in Newfoundland and Labrador held their Rangers.

In dozens of communities throughout Newfoundland and Labrador this week Newfoundlander the force ceases to exist are saying goodbye to the men who for fifteen years have been peace officers, government officials and friends. Tomorrow the force ceases to exist. The familiar khaki uniform will be replaced by the drab brown uniform of the RCMP.

Primarily peace officers, the Rangers came to be looked upon as much more than that in the isolated settlements which came under their jurisdiction. They carried side arms, but never for once had to draw them. They fought through freezing seas in small boats to bring first aid when medical services were unavailable along the jagged coastline. They slogged overland in winter by dog sled and snowshoes to bring sick or injured people to hospital.

They battled forest fires, patrolled fish and game areas, and performed countless other tasks of government administration. Although the uniform will disappear, their traditions will remain. So will Ranger personnel, many of whom are joining the RCMP and continuing their present duties.

CONCLUSION

Though they existed for only fifteen years, the Newfoundland Rangers earned a place in the province's history. Rangers also secured a warm place in the hearts of ordinary Newfoundlanders.

At a time when Responsible Government had been suspended, Rangers had tremendous powers in outports throughout Newfoundland and Labrador. But there are no known cases of that power being abused. Rather there are many examples and stories of Rangers using their extensive powers to help the impoverished, the needy and the sick.

While they carried side-arms they were not feared by the public but respected. This respect was earned through consistent professionalism and courtesy. Even the smugglers and poachers respected the Rangers. They might have tried to outwit them with contraband liquor or illegally gotten game, but they still respected the Ranger. Witness the struggles that the civilian search party went through to find Ranger Danny Corcoran on the barrens of the Northern Peninsula.

Harold Horwood writes that the "decision to replace the Rangers by the RCMP (in 1950) was made by the Smallwood Government for purely financial reasons." The Rangers were not disbanded because the RCMP was a superior force. Of course, the RCMP had helped train the first Rangers.

It apparently cost more to maintain a provincial police force than to "rent Mounties from the Federal Government." While the Opposition Members of the House of Assembly resisted the dissolution of the Ranger Force, the Liberal majority held the day.

Rangers were given the opportunity to enter the RCMP provided they were found physically fit and could pass the entrance exams. But there was no outright guarantee of admittance.

A further indignity heaped on the Rangers was that those who would join the RCMP did so at a reduced rank. For example, a Sergeant in the Rangers would become a Corporal in the RCMP.

Former Ranger and author Cyril Goodyear discusses the RCMP's swallowing of the Ranger Force in his book *The Road to Nowhere.*

Goodyear says that without "adequate notice or explanation we were summoned to St. John's to be examined and assessed to see if we were suitable for engagement in the RCMP."

According to Goodyear, in a letter dated July 4, 1950, Chief Ranger E. L. Martin advised all Rangers that he had received a letter from then Attorney General, Leslie R. Curtis, advising that the RCMP would be offering all Rangers positions in that Force effective August 1, 1950, but at reduced ranks.

Goodyear goes on to write that Rangers were instructed to reply immediately and that should any Ranger refuse to join the RCMP the provincial government would not assist them in obtaining other employment.

Cyril Goodyear was one Ranger who had little choice but to join the RCMP. He was married with a pregnant spouse. He needed to maintain employment. So, he signed up for a five year contract. Goodyear was one of 55 Rangers who entered the RCMP in August 1950. Surely, the intricate knowledge the Rangers had of outport Newfoundland was a great assistance to Canada's national force as it began to police Newfoundland and Labrador.

On July 27, 1950, Chief Ranger Martin issued discharges to all Rangers accompanied by a letter of farewell. The Ranger Force at that time numbered 77 officers and men, Horwood says.

The Newfoundland Ranger Force officially came to an end on July 31, 1950. This was just fifteen months after Newfoundland had become a province. Cyril Goodyear writes in The Road to Nowhere that the disbandment of the Rangers could not have been planned in just fifteen months. He believes that the RCMP's absorption of the Ranger Force was planned during the discussions over the Terms of Union between Canada and Newfoundland.

Ches Parsons (#152) recalls that when he was first serving as an RCMP officer his first posting was in Placentia. He remembers that the newly minted Mounties were poorly equipped.

"I arrived in Placentia on August 8, 1950. There was myself, Walter Green and William Walsh. We had no RCMP uniforms, the only identification we had was an RCMP hat badge held by Green. Walsh had a uniform, but it was too big for him. I served a couple of weeks with no RCMP uniform," Ches recalls.

Research Complications

When we decided to write this book, the Executive of the Newfoundland Ranger Force Association were pleased with the decision and gave their full endorsement.

First observation would lead one to believe that with the Rangers record of committing practically everything to paper, retrieving the most basic records would be found in the Provincial Archives or some other location. Not so. As a matter of fact not one "Application for Engagement" was found by co-author Ches Parsons, despite much digging. The question as to why is not understood and leaves the matter open to speculation.

Without such records, the task of determining what community or settlement the members were from and who the parents were created a task of major proportions. Sources such as Ranger Force Association Newsletters, the 1911, 1921, and 1935 Census of Newfoundland plus the Internet had to be utilized. Eight members did not have a known address. Tracing friends or relatives of deceased members, especially those who moved out of the province, and those who made no effort to keep in touch, demanded lots of perseverance. Also complicating matters were initials and surnames. For example: Winsor vs Windsor; Stickland vs Strickland; Clarke vs Clark, McCue vs McHugh and many others. In the matter of initials, one member who had only one initial and served a very short time still has not been identified.

Because of the complications as outlined, hundreds and hundreds of phone calls were made and numerous e-mails and regular postage letters sent. Ches Parsons took on the monumental task of tracking down leads on the ex-Rangers. He spent hours on the phone, at his own expense.

Says Ches:

> "With respect to the phone calls, I can say that I was greeted with understanding and cheerfulness. All, with one or two exceptions, were eager to assist and in many cases called back at their own expense to furnish the information required. Photos were sent or collected as they became available. I will not soon forget some of the phone calls, and to show why, will tell briefly of two. I obtained a U.S. phone number, off the Internet, bearing the surname of a deceased member. Explaining the purpose of the call I was greeted with the expression: "I can't believe this, I can't believe this". Long pause. "I am the grandson of that member and will have my Dad get in touch with you as soon as possible." We had a long conversation as I had researched his Newfoundland roots fairly extensively. Another one was to a lady who had agreed to check on one or two ex-members who had lived in or near her community. On three or more occasions I called her to find out what she had learned or to relate what I had obtained since last talking to her. On the next call her husband answered the phone and I asked if I could talk to his spouse. The next words I heard as he shouted out to her were: "That old fellow who keeps calling you all the time is on the phone". I suppressed a chuckle as much as I could but am still wondering what triggered the assessment of my age."

Ches's persistence paid dividends and so we were able to present at least some biographical information on each of the 204 enlisted men who served as Rangers.

Remembering Comrades

In mid-June 1968, seventy ex-Rangers met in St. John's to hold a two-day reunion. At that time a Newfoundland Ranger Force Association was begun. They hold regular meetings and issue a newsletter.

A plaque bearing the names of all 204 Rangers was unveiled on the grounds of Colonial Building in St. John's on September 20, 1980. Colonial Building had been the seat of government when Newfoundland was an independent country and it seems a fitting home for a monument to the Rangers.

In 1991 the Ranger Force Association established a scholarship at Memorial University of Newfoundland. On December 20 that year a group of ex-Rangers presented the first amount for the scholarship fund to then University President Arthur May. The scholarship fund has grown to the point that it will help fund two students each year in perpetuity.

In 2004, the St. John's firm of G.J. Cahill helped unveil a monument and display to the Rangers on its premises. The site occupied by Cahill's on Waterford Bridge Road across from Corpus Christi Church was the site of Ranger Headquarters from 1943 - 1950. The Ranger Force Association cooperated with Cahill's to establish a picture board display and monument.

But more than monuments, displays or even the scholarship fund, it is the actions of the Rangers that ensure they will not be forgotten. The Rangers' feats, achievements and selfless dedication to serving ordinary Newfoundlanders will survive the passing of time. The Rangers were absorbed by the RCMP, not replaced.